PRAISE FOR ORDINARY C
EXTRAORDINARY SIGNS

"This Saint Paul Evangelization Institute training manual presents the biblical basis for the relationship between healing and evangelization with accuracy and depth of understanding. The practical instructions it offers are as good and thorough and easy to use as any I have seen anywhere. Everything about this resource is faithfully Catholic to the core. I enthusiastically recommend this book, which will help many Catholics to proclaim the gospel in the power of the Holy Spirit."
—**Dr. Peter S. Williamson,** Adam Cardinal Maida Chair of Sacred Scripture, Sacred Heart Major Seminary

"This book is not only good—it's outstanding! It includes little-known sources and quotations from Church authorities and makes the case for healing in evangelization in a compelling way. Catholics, especially priests and lay leaders, need to read this."
—**Dr. Mary Healy,** professor of Scripture, Sacred Heart Major Seminary and author of *Healing: Bringing the Gift of God's Mercy to the World*

"With sound teaching, remarkable healing testimonies, and tested practical advice, this easy-to-read manual will prepare any reader to pray for healing with confidence. It also emphasizes an important and essential element to the New Evangelization: the power of signs and wonders to draw people to Christ and the Church."
—**Bert Ghezzi,** author of *The Power of Daily Prayer*

"St. Paul said it: 'The kingdom of God does not consist in talk but in power' (1 Corinthians 4:20). We all know that Jesus and the apostles preached about the kingdom of God and even demonstrated the powerful works of the kingdom through healing, miracles, and the casting out of evil spirits. But plain, ordinary, everyday Christians are also called to performed miracles and healings—to demonstrate the kingdom's healing power.

"This manual shows you how. The teaching is practical, clear, and accessible to anyone who can read. It is faithful to Church teaching. And when it is applied, it works! It has been tested through the ages. When the works of the kingdom accompany the words of the kingdom, heaven touches earth and eternal life opens up. King Jesus is, right now, healing the broken world through his body on earth, the Church. That's you!"

—**Al Kresta,** president and CEO of Ave Maria Radio and host of *Kresta in the Afternoon*

"While the Church teaches us to 'earnestly desire the spiritual gifts' (1 Corinthians 14:1), the vast majority of Catholics remain uninformed. This manual makes a valuable contribution to understanding and using the spiritual gifts in the work of evangelization."

—**Dave Nodar,** founder and director of ChristLife

"The wait for a theologically sound and detailed guide for Catholics on how to pray for healing to demonstrate the truth of the gospel is over. In this bold and faith-inspiring manual, Dawson and Hornbacher offer the tools and wisdom necessary to pray for healing with astonishing results. The teaching in this book is so powerful that if only a small percentage of readers faithfully put into practice what the authors suggest, street evangelization will never be the same. A superb achievement—highly recommended."

—**Fr. Mathias Thelen, STL,** senior leader of Encounter Ministries and pastor of St. Patrick Church, Brighton, Michigan

"I love this book. Every Catholic engaged in evangelization can benefit from it. You will be instructed by sound teaching and practical wisdom gained through years of experience. You will be inspired to trust in God's

power to change hearts and heal bodies. If you are willing to expand the parameters of how God can use you, you will love this book too!"
—**Neal Lozano,** author of *Unbound: A Practical Guide to Deliverance* and founder of Heart of the Father Ministries

"I am very impressed with the material the Saint Paul Evangelization Institute is developing, and this *Healing in Evangelization* manual is no exception. There aren't many voices today that truly teach and preach the 'full gospel,' including the challenging parts, in a thoroughly Catholic context. May their tribe increase!"
—**Ralph Martin, STD,** president of Renewal Ministries

"Jesus spent approximately twenty-five percent of his time healing and yet for many Catholic leaders, integrating healing effectively into parish evangelization ministry seems to be a difficult task. The Saint Paul Evangelization Institute provides an imminently practical and accessible training manual in *Ordinary Christians, Extraordinary Signs.* Weaving insight from Scripture, the lives of the saints, and the rich tradition of the Church, this manual is truly a wonderful gift to the Catholic Church. This practical, reflective, and accessible manual should be in the hands of all Catholic leaders who seek to evangelize the world for Jesus Christ."
—**Julianne Stanz,** director of Discipleship and Leadership Development, Diocese of Green Bay, and consultant to the USCCB Committee on Evangelization and Catechesis

"Without a doubt, the Saint Paul Evangelization Institute has created one of the most critical resources for the Church's mission today: a comprehensive and practical guide to recovering the explicitly healing dimensions of evangelization. Programs and processes cannot, by themselves, bear fruit, but men and women intentionally cooperating with the *power* of the Holy Spirit will transform the world in Christ. The work of the Saint Paul Evangelization Institute, and this manual in particular, are indispensable in raising up a generation of such empowered missionary disciples."
—**Deacon Keith Strohm,** executive director, M3 Ministries

Ordinary Christians Extraordinary Signs

Healing in Evangelization

STEVE DAWSON AND MARK J. HORNBACHER

FOREWORD BY ARCHBISHOP ALLEN VIGNERON

Published by The Word Among Us Press
7115 Guilford Drive, Suite 100
Frederick, Maryland 21704

23 22 21 20 19   1 2 3 4 5

ISBN: 978-1-59325-005-8
eISBN: 978-1-59325-007-2

Cover design by Suzanne Earl, David Crosson

Made and printed in the United States of America

Library of Congress Control Number: 2019932480

Ecclesial approval for publication granted by the Most Reverend Allen H. Vigneron, Archbishop of Detroit, 10 December 2018.

This ecclesial approval confirms that a publication does not contain errors concerning the presentation of Catholic faith and morals. No implication is contained herein that the one granting the approval agrees with the contents, opinions, or statements expressed.

Given at Detroit, Michigan, on this tenth day of December, in the year of our Lord, two thousand eighteen.

+The Most Reverend Allen H. Vigneron
Archbishop of Detroit

CONTENTS

FOREWORD

In considering how best to help others be prepared to read this volume, my thoughts recurred again and again to our recent celebration of the centenary of the apparition of the Blessed Virgin Mary to the three children at Fatima. The connection may seem a bit obscure at first, but to me it shines out clearly.

Our Lord sent his Mother to Fatima in the role of an evangelist. At a very dark and fearful time in the history of the world, she came proclaiming the good news of the invincible reign of Christ the King as the foundation for the peace that mankind was in such desperate need of. And in imitation of her Son's own announcement of the good news during his earthly ministry, the Holy Mother of God called for prayer and repentance as the road to be traveled in order to take possession of the saving graces won for us by our Savior. Do we not hear in her message to Lucia, Jacinta, and Francisco an echo of his words: "The kingdom of God is at hand; repent and believe in the gospel" (Mark 1:15)? And just as the Lord, as part of his mission as an evangelist, commissioned others to join him in being evangelists themselves after he had evangelized them, so too at Fatima, our Lady commissioned the three children to share with others the message of hope she shared with them. Evangelized by the Blessed Virgin, Lucia, Jacinta, and Francisco in their turn became evangelists.

Upon reflection the parallels are even more striking. For, like the original proclamation of the good news by Jesus, Our Lady's work as an evangelist was accompanied by "signs and wonders" (see Acts 4:30). Her service as one sent by God to proclaim his gracious will to the twentieth century was, like the evangelizing mission of the apostles of the first century, confirmed thereby (see, among others, Mark 16:20 and Hebrew 2:4).

An attentive reading of the role of our Blessed Mother in the history of the Church leads us to recognize that the patterns we discern in her evangelizing at Fatima can be identified in other missions entrusted to her by her Son. At Guadalupe she was a powerful agent for the evangelizing of the native peoples of America. She commissioned Juan Diego, in turn, to be her collaborator in this great work, and what else is her image on Juan Diego's *tilma* but the sign and wonder that confirmed the good news of the tender and compassionate love offered, as our Lady said, by "the true God who is the author of life, the creator of all things, the Lord of heaven and earth, present everywhere" to those the world considers the least and the littlest.

Again, at Lourdes in the middle of the nineteenth century, Our Lady appeared to one of God's little ones with the good news that the Lord is not far away and uncaring as the sophisticated rationalists of the day asserted, but is among us, is one of us, and is ever near to us in our trials and sorrows as our Savior. Here, too, the Blessed Virgin commissioned the Lord's humble handmaid, Bernadette Soubirous, the daughter of a man who made his living by carting refuse, to hand on to the world the saving message that the Blessed Virgin was sent to entrust to her. Among the most prominent signs and wonders which the Lord worked to confirm the authenticity of this message have been the many healings that have taken place at the Grotto of Massabielle. And rightly so.

What I infer from these marvelous interventions of the Blessed Virgin in the life of the Church is that "signs and wonders" and "the proclamation of God's saving word" make a most fit pairing in the ecology of grace.

As the principal pastor of the Catholic Church in the Archdiocese of Detroit, I heard clearly what our recent Archdiocesan Synod on the New Evangelization said about this "duo" of the New Covenant. After listening to the insights of the members of the synod about the place of signs and wonders in the mission of evangelization, I gave expression to this conviction: As it was when the apostles first spread the gospel,

> so today we look for the proclamation of the good news to be accompanied by signs and wonders that visibly demonstrate God's love and convince people that Jesus Christ is truly alive. We have been given a prison-shaking

Savior, a deliverer who sets captives free! Signs, small and great, are a normal part of the Christian life. Our focus is not on the signs themselves, but on the risen Lord Jesus to whom they point. "By the power at work within us [he] is able to do far more abundantly than all that we ask or imagine (Eph 3:20). (Pastoral Letter, *Unleash the Gospel*, 4.1.3)

Just such a conviction—that it is reasonable to expect signs and wonders to accompany the proclamation of the Gospel in the New Evangelization—has led the leaders of the St. Paul Evangelization Institute to prayerfully to discern the role that prayers for healing would play in their ministry. They have been moved to take up joyfully the mission of sharing the light of the Good News of salvation with a world that stubbornly insists on staying stuck "in darkness and in the shadow of death" (Luke 1:79), and so must be shaken out of its deafness and blindness to the life that is the "light of men . . . [offered in the] grace and truth [that has come] through Jesus Christ" (John 1:4, 17).

All of us in the Church can assist them with our prayers that they persevere in undertaking their service of the gospel. They carry out this service, not relying on themselves but placing their confidence in the power of the Holy Spirit, and taking up this great work in unconditional communion with the Church and her pastors. Let us be one with them in asking the intercession of the Mother of God to bring forth much good fruit for the Lord's glory and the salvation of souls in all we do to advance the New Evangelization.

The Most Reverend Allen H. Vigneron
Archbishop of Detroit

ACKNOWLEDGMENTS

First and foremost, all glory and praise to God, and to Jesus Christ, Our Lord! We're not worthy of the opportunities he's given us, and the mercy he never stops pouring out for us. We're also very grateful to everyone who helped us in one way or another in the writing of this book, including but not limited to:

Archbishop Allen Vigneron, not only for writing the foreword, but for his encouragement and support throughout the years.

Dr. Mary Healy, for her critical role as a theological advisor for this project and a friend of the Institute.

Maria Libey, for allowing us to share her story of healing, and for her Mary-like example to us of pondering in her heart the great things God has done for her.

All the Saint Paul Street Evangelization team leaders and evangelists who encouraged us with their stories of miraculous healing.

We also want to thank many people for their behind-the-scenes counsel, input, and help editing and revising: Rev. Charles Fox, Rev. Mathias Thelen, Patrick Reis, Neal Lozano, Bert Ghezzi, Adam Janke, Maria Dawson, John Michalik, and others. Thanks also to everyone at The Word Among Us Press for getting this book to print.

Lastly, we want to honor St. Paul, the great apostle and evangelist, and Our Lady of Guadalupe, Star of the New Evangelization, for showing us how faith should rest in the power of God. May they help us trust and welcome anew God's power, to bear much fruit for him.

INTRODUCTION

I stood in the front doorway of my house and watched as our dinner guest ambled up the pathway that led to the porch.

"Maria, what's wrong? You're limping!" I called as I stepped off the porch to meet her. I hadn't noticed the limp before; she must have injured herself since the last time I saw her.

"Oh, that's nothing," she said. "It's a birth defect. One of my legs is two inches shorter than the other, but it's no big deal. I've had it my entire life." I helped her up the two steps to the porch.

"Hey, I've been praying for people who are injured or have other physical conditions, and sometimes they get healed. Maybe we can pray and God will heal your birth defect," I said.

Maria looked at me quizzically and shook her head, waving her hand dismissively. But something inside me told me to persist. "Why not just try it? What do we have to lose?" I asked.

Maria laughed. "Steve, if you really want to pray for me, ask God to heal my sleep because I haven't been able to sleep properly for a long time."

I nodded. "Come on in."

I had only known Maria for a couple of months. She was a charming, devout, eighty-six-year-old woman who was born in Brazil but lived in the United States most of her life. She had stumbled upon my office one fall afternoon, and we had talked evangelization for a while. Then in her warm, unassuming way, she had pressed to meet my family. This was her second visit to my home.

During dinner, Maria told us more about her physical ailments. She had had brain surgery several years earlier, and since then her sleep had been very much disrupted, and she had not been able to dream.

Also, all her life Maria walked with a limp because her legs were different lengths. As a girl and young woman, it didn't bother her much, but she would have her dresses hemmed at a slant so that they would not appear crooked. As she grew older, she became more unsteady on her feet and often relied on a cane. She found that she could no longer walk long distances easily or stand for extended periods. A shoe insert helped alleviate other leg problems caused by the condition.

Soon after dessert, I announced that it was time to pray for Maria. She and I went into another room, and I began by invoking the Holy Spirit. After a minute of quiet, I asked, in the name of Jesus, that God restore Maria to normal restful sleep patterns. Maria told me later that at that moment, she had felt God's presence and peace.

Although all evening I had been eager to pray for Maria's healing, I hadn't planned to push the leg issue. Now somehow I couldn't resist. "Why don't I pray for your leg now, that God heals it so you can walk better?"

Maria shook her head. "Steve, I don't believe that God is going to heal me of that."

"Why not?"

"Because I don't have faith that God would *want* to heal my leg. I believe that he *can*, but why *would* he? Why would he heal me now at eighty-six, when I've managed fine my whole life with the condition he gave me at birth?"

"That's okay that you don't have faith, Maria," I said. "Think about the centurion who came to Jesus on behalf of his sick servant. Jesus healed that servant and attributed the healing to the *centurion's* faith, not the servant's. Let *me* have faith for you."

Maria looked at me for several moments, then reluctantly shrugged her consent. I knew she was humoring me, but I was going for it anyway. She was seated, and I stood in front of her and picked up both of her feet. When I put the heels together, it was clear that her left leg was considerably shorter. I simply prayed, "In the name of Jesus, leg, be healed!"

I looked down at her feet, still in my hands. The heels now lined up. In the blink of an eye, her legs were the same length.

"Maria, I think your legs are the same length now. I mean, I didn't see one grow, but they look the same to me now. What do you think?"

Maria looked down at her feet, then lifted them straight at the knees and rotated her ankles. "I don't know," she said.

"Ok, let's measure them." I darted to the kitchen and returned with a tape measure. Maria stood, and I knelt down beside her.

"Thirty-one inches . . . and . . . thirty-one inches!"

She seemed puzzled, and I urged her to walk around. She acknowledged that there was something different about her legs. I ushered her back to the kitchen where I measured her legs twice more and asked my wife to take a fourth set of measurements, just to be sure.

We were in a state of stunned disbelief. We did not doubt God's power, but had we really expected him to work in this way? Even I, who had put on the pressure to pray for Maria's leg, could barely believe it. Maria kept asking why God would do it.

Maria told me later that during the healing prayer session she was sure I was pulling on her leg. I assured her that I wasn't, but she insisted that she had felt a distinct pulling sensation while I was praying. Early in the morning the day after the healing, Maria was awakened by a pain in her left leg. She said it was "as if the muscles wanted to stretch." The pain disappeared later in the day, and that evening Maria attended a prayer service during which she was able to stand until the end without being worried that she would fall. Maria's gait is so much improved that she no longer needs to use a cane.

Maria was sure that God had made her leg grow two inches, and I was convinced too. Still, I wanted further medical verification, an "official" measurement, something more than I with my workshop tape measure could do. So I suggested to Maria that she obtain a statement from her doctor. Using a specialized device, her physiotherapist measured her legs and documented them both to be 80 centimeters in length.

A ✝ Ω

When I came to you, brethren, I did not come proclaiming to you the testimony of God in lofty words or wisdom. For I decided to know nothing among you except Jesus Christ and him crucified. And I was with you in weakness and in much fear and trembling; and my speech and my message were not in plausible words of wisdom, but in demonstration of the Spirit and of power, that your faith might not rest in the wisdom of men but in the power of God.

—The First Letter of St. Paul to the Corinthians 2:1-5

When writing to the Corinthians, St. Paul, our patron, makes clear that his proclamation of the gospel to them was not mere intellectual persuasion. There was something about his testimony to Christ that was more than words. And it wasn't just that the words he was speaking were true. As he puts it, his preaching was "in demonstration of the Spirit and of power" (1 Corinthians 2:4).

What exactly does this mean? Many Scripture scholars, old and new, have commented on this passage, including St. Thomas Aquinas and the great Jesuit commentator Cornelius à Lapide.[1] Reading the text in the light of the context of the rest of the letter, and of St. Paul's other letters, and indeed with the whole of Scripture, they generally find two basic meanings here.

The first meaning is that Paul's proclamation of the gospel of the crucified Christ, itself, had power that was both manifest in him (the preacher) and in the Corinthians (the listeners). When the gospel is preached in the Holy Spirit, God manifests himself in his power to transform hearts and minds unto salvation. We see this in many places in the Scriptures. In St. Paul's letter to the Romans, for example, he says, "I am not ashamed of the gospel: it is the power of God for salvation to every one who has faith, to the Jew first and also to the Greek" (1:16). In his First Letter to the Corinthians he writes, "The word of the cross is folly to those who are perishing, but to us who are being saved it is the power of God" (1:18).[2] And also, "The kingdom of God does not consist in talk but in power" (4:20).[3] In the Gospels and in the Acts of the Apostles, we see Jesus and the apostles preaching with power—with a manifest authority or boldness, and with the ability to convince minds and change hearts in unexpected ways.

The second meaning of the passage, just as clear as the first, is that along with the proclamation of the gospel there came also signs and wonders: healings, the expulsion of demons, and other miracles.

Sacred Scripture greatly supports this second meaning. As we know, miraculous healings and other manifestations of divine power filled the ministry of Christ. In turn, many miraculous signs confirmed the apostles' preaching. After the scriptural record, we have the record of the early Church: we've all read or heard stories of the great martyrs and confessors of the faith whose deeds were accompanied by signs and wonders—healings, exorcisms, and remarkable miracles. Going further in Church history, even into modern times, we're aware of many saints for whom God performed miraculous healings and amazing signs.

Jesus, the apostles, St. Paul, the martyrs, and the saints—they all performed signs and wonders to build up the kingdom of God. But are we aware that other people did too? Are we aware that in the early Church, a very great number of *ordinary* Christians also performed such deeds?[4] Do we know that the New Testament supports the notion that ordinary Christians will perform miracles?

The evangelist extraordinaire St. Paul, who told the ordinary Christians of Corinth to imitate him (see 1 Corinthians 4:16, 11:1), preached with a "demonstration of the Spirit and of power" (2:4). Is it possible that we are supposed to imitate him, too? As we have seen, this "demonstration of the Spirit and of power" includes signs, wonders, miracles, healings. If the greatest evangelist after Christ used these wondrous means to bring home the good news to the hearts and minds of his listeners, might we be called to use them too, as members of the Church commissioned to "preach the gospel to the whole creation" (Mark 16:15)? Could it be that signs and wonders are meant to be abundant today too, as they were for the early Church?

Furthermore, how much more fruit might *our* evangelization efforts bear if they were accompanied by miraculous signs? If preaching the gospel and miraculous signs are so intimately linked, might such signs help *us* get the gospel message across to our dechristianized culture?

But, you say, *surely we can't conjure up miracles on our own; the Lord bestows them as he chooses.* Well, then, do we dare *ask* the Lord that we might receive such gifts? Might he even *want* us to ask him and expect in faith that he will act?

Some time ago, we at Saint Paul Evangelization Institute (SPEI) began asking ourselves these same kinds of questions. We saw that signs and wonders were important for the evangelizing efforts of Christ, the apostles, the early Church, and the saints—and we had heard of modern cases, but that did not add up to a clear conclusion that God wanted *us* to make use of such signs today in our apostolate. However, we did *desire* to see signs and wonders in evangelization today—not because we wanted to see miracles but because we wanted to see more hearts open to the gospel. So we continued to study, research, and discern the question, seeking the counsel of respected clergy, and we received the go-ahead to begin praying that God would perform miracles for the spreading of the gospel.

So we prayed for physical healing with people who needed it, and we started to see some small things happen—like people with discomfort or pain feeling relieved. Around that same time, we found out that one of our teams in Ohio had prayed for healing for a man who had been confined to a wheelchair for seven years from an injury and complications from surgery, and who also had arthritis and cancer. The team had met the man while street evangelizing and invited him to a Nightfever event that evening with Eucharistic adoration. The man was healed: he began to walk on his own, his pain and arthritis went away, and the cancer went into remission; he also began to go to Mass.

News of this healing sent us into deeper discernment, seeking the direction of those with experience of fruitful prayer for healing. And we began asking the Lord that if it was his will, he would confirm our growing feeling that we ought to teach this through the apostolate.

The thing was that these miracles were still mostly muscular-skeletal. A person would have pain, we would pray, and the pain would go away. But how could we prove it? We wanted something more substantial, something we could consider a sign of confirmation that using and teaching healing in evangelization was what God desired for SPEI.

That's where Maria's story comes in; her miracle was different. You do not simply *imagine* a leg growing two inches. An additional two inches of bone, muscle, nerves, skin, and tendons are not the result of someone's subjective impression. Maria's healing was a *creative* miracle; something new was added to her physical body to make her whole. And those two inches are measurable.

During that time of becoming more acquainted with the workings of God's power, that creative miracle was what we needed. We received it as a sign from God that He desires *healing in evangelization* for the Church today, both in SPEI and in the wider Church. Maria's miracle helped confirm for us that "signs and wonders" are not just for helping the early Church to grow and spread, but also for building up the two-thousand-year-old Church in a post-Christian world.

Since we are now convinced that we are called to seek and exercise the spiritual gifts (especially healing) in our evangelization efforts, we have put together this *Healing in Evangelization* training manual. By it, we want to give you a sound scriptural, historical, and magisterial (Church teaching) basis for ordinary Christians being instruments of healing and miraculous signs for building up the kingdom of God. We also provide a simple, practical, and effective approach to healing prayer, guidance on seeking this gift, and notes on applying this approach to public evangelization.

Chapter 1 demonstrates that healing in evangelization is based in Scripture (focusing especially on the ministry of Christ) and in Church history. Chapter 2 shows how the teaching authority of the Church supports the notion that ordinary Christians can perform miraculous deeds of healing, and how the unique times in which we live call for them. Chapter 3 gives a four-step process for healing prayer, and chapter 4 addresses praying to receive the gift of healing. Chapter 5 puts healing prayer into the context of publicly sharing the gospel. Finally, the manual includes appendices that treat certain important topics in greater depth, answer frequently asked questions, and provide instruction on praying for the healing of specific kinds of conditions.

One may ask, "How can you teach someone to heal?" While miraculous healings do not come from us but are gifts of God's omnipotent power, there remain human aspects that can be taught. The sixteenth-century evangelization efforts of St. Francis Xavier give us an amazing precedent for "teaching" miraculous healing. St. Francis was among the first seven men to join St. Ignatius of Loyola's new religious community, the Society of Jesus, and he experienced a call to evangelize in the Far East. While he was there, the Lord worked through him many signs of healing, and he passed this gift to others: on at least one occasion, St. Francis trained little children to visit the sick, teach them the creed, and cure them by their prayer.[5]

Another question many might have is, "Why have the miraculous manifestations of God's power seen in the early Church diminished so profoundly?" We consider this question in chapter 1, and posit a related, provocative one of our own in chapter 2: "What is it about our world today that would make the regular manifestation of signs and wonders especially appropriate?" We make the case that today's "signs of the times" call for a new outpouring of the Spirit in the form of healings and miracles, and that God desires that we humbly seek these gifts as power-boosters to evangelization.

However, we are far from suggesting that extraordinary gifts of this kind are the most important gifts, or that they should be sought for their own sake. And certainly not everyone who asks will be granted them. Our aim here is simply to encourage you to expand your horizons, to tap into all your resources. After all, we serve the all-powerful God, and God desires that the whole world submit to the authority of his love much more than do we, his hands and feet. Will he not supply to us the perfect means to tell the world about him? We must only seek in earnest to do his will and trust that what he grants is best. And if he desires to grant a "demonstration of the Spirit and of power" (1 Corinthians 2:4), let us be ready to receive it!

We hope that through this book you will be inspired to cultivate continually a spirit of active trust and reliance on God, so that as you do the work of evangelization, you may act boldly, not from your own resources, but from the Lord's, without whom you can do nothing (see John 15:5) and with whom you can do all things (see Philippians 4:13).

Chapter 1

THE SACRED SCRIPTURES AND CHURCH HISTORY

When Jesus entered Peter's house, he saw his mother-in-law lying sick with a fever; he touched her hand, and the fever left her, and she rose and served him. That evening they brought to him many who were possessed with demons; and he cast out the spirits with a word, and healed all who were sick. This was to fulfill what was spoken by the prophet Isaiah, "He took our infirmities and bore our diseases."

—The Gospel According to Matthew 8:14-17

In referring to the passage from Isaiah chapter 53, the evangelist Matthew shows that God intended the mission of the Messiah to include physical healing. In both the Old and New Testaments, healing (and other miraculous events) are most often depicted as signs and expressions of God's power, compassion, saving presence, and loving-kindness for his people. This corresponds to a parallel biblical truth: sickness, suffering, and death, though ultimately included under the providential plan of God and potentially corrective and redemptive,[6] are signs of the oppressive dominion of sin and the devil.[7]

It should come as no surprise, then, that the preaching of the gospel and the healing of the sick should go closely together. Again and again in the Old Testament, God is revealed as healer; and he promises, through a Messiah, to come and deliver his people from, among other things, *illness*. And as mentioned, illness is, directly or indirectly, a work of the devil. As the apostle John wrote, "The reason the Son of God appeared was to destroy the works of the devil" (1 John 3:8).[8] All of this puts works of healing in a central place within the gospel message.

Accordingly, the preaching and teaching ministry of Jesus Christ is *filled* with healings, exorcisms, and other miracles; so much so that they appear as a central feature of his ministry.[9] Indeed, the Lord's preaching and his healings and exorcisms are typically interspersed or placed very closely to one another in the Gospel narratives. In the first chapter of the Gospel of Mark, for example, after Jesus' baptism, fasting in the desert, and the calling of the first disciples, there follows in rapid succession an exorcism, a number of healings, a preaching tour, and another healing, all before another healing in chapter 2. At times, preaching and healing or exorcisms are even mentioned in the same breath—as if they were two parts of the same thing: "And he went about all Galilee, teaching in their synagogues and preaching the gospel of the kingdom and healing every disease and every infirmity among the people" (Matthew 4:23).

And this is just in the Gospels. There are also a number of important verses in Acts and the epistles which tie healing and other signs closely to evangelization.[10] Indeed, when all relevant texts are considered, it is clear: *in the Sacred Scriptures, the preaching of the gospel and the performing of healings and other signs go intimately together.*

In the following pages, we will more closely look at the special relationship between evangelization and healing in the Scriptures, especially in the ministry of Jesus; but briefly, also in the ministry of the apostles. Afterward, we will look and see how the history of the Church also reflects this special relationship. Pope Emeritus Benedict XVI, in his book *Jesus of Nazareth*, says, ". . . the *evangelium*, the Gospel, is not just informative speech, but **performative speech**—not just the imparting of information, but action, efficacious power that enters into the world to save and transform."[11] While this surely means transforming hearts, minds, and souls, Scripture and Church history tell us that it also means healing bodies.

Signs of the Kingdom of God

And they came to Jericho; and as he was leaving Jericho with his disciples and a great multitude, Bartimaeus, a blind beggar, the son of Timaeus, was sitting by the roadside. And when he heard that it was Jesus of Nazareth, he began to cry out and say, "Jesus, Son of David, have mercy on me!" And many rebuked him, telling him to be silent; but he cried out all the more, "Son of David, have mercy on me!" And Jesus stopped and said, "Call him." And they called the blind man, saying to him, "Take heart; rise, he is calling you." And throwing off his mantle he sprang up and came to Jesus. And Jesus said to him, "What do you want me to do for you?" And the blind man said to him, "Master, let me receive my sight." And Jesus said to him, "Go your way; your faith has made you well." And immediately he received his sight and followed him on the way.

—The Gospel According to Mark 10:46-52

Up until this point in the Gospel of Mark, Jesus had tried to keep his identity as the Messiah secret (see Mark 8:30). But now that he is on his way to Jerusalem to undergo his passion and death, he allows the messianic title "Son of David" to be applied to him, while others try to silence it.[12]

In this scene, then, we see highlighted the profound connection between healing and the coming of the Messiah.[13] The coming of Jesus Christ, foretold by the Old Testament prophets, is accompanied by healings. The kingdom has truly come near, for the Davidic King is entering his city to ascend his throne;[14] and he marks that entrance with a healing.

But why *should* he mark it with a healing? What does the gospel have to do with healing?

Think about it in this way: *What is the gospel?* During his earthly ministry, Jesus revealed that *in him, the saving promises of God are fulfilled; the kingdom of God is near*, and faith and repentance are the proper responses to this message. After Pentecost, the apostles, for their part, preached what is essentially the same content: *Jesus is Lord, Son of God, Savior, and Anointed King/Messiah*, who is returning; and faith and repentance are the proper responses.

So, in a nutshell, the gospel is this: Jesus Christ, the Son of God, is King. But what is it like to experience the reign of such a king? Jesus answers this question for us. In Capernaum, to inaugurate his preaching ministry, Jesus reads from chapter 61 of the prophet Isaiah, "The Spirit of the Lord is upon me, because he has anointed me to preach good news to the poor. He has sent me to proclaim release to the captives and recovering of sight to the blind, to set at liberty those who are oppressed, to proclaim the acceptable year of the Lord" (Luke 4:18-19). Again, when verifying his identity for John the Baptist, Jesus describes his mission similarly, alluding again to prophecies of Isaiah: "The blind receive their sight and the lame walk, lepers are cleansed and the deaf hear, and the dead are raised up, and the poor have good news preached to them" (Matthew 11:5).[15]

Though Jesus was referencing Isaiah in both cases, he was also indirectly referencing a large body of Old Testament prophecies concerning God, the Messiah, and the Messianic Age, all of which tell us about the loving character of God and the healing and liberating nature of his kingdom.[16]

So, again, we ask: What does it mean to experience the kingdom of God in Jesus Christ? And we answer confidently, from the Scriptures: freedom from bondage! Deliverance from oppression! Health and life instead of sickness and death! Good news instead of hopelessness! . . . *In other words, salvation!*

Now we know, of course, that this salvation is primarily spiritual— deliverance from the bondage of sin. But in the ministry of Jesus and the apostles, again and again, it is clear that healings as well as exorcisms and other deliverances of the body are also included, for they are placed side-by-side with the proclamation of salvation through repentance from sin.[17] They are component parts of a complete salvation which is reserved for the end of time when "he will wipe away every tear from their eyes, and death shall be no more, neither shall there be mourning nor crying nor pain any more, for the former things have passed away" (Revelation 21:4). In this eternal Jerusalem, "no inhabitant will say, 'I am sick'; the people who dwell there will be forgiven their iniquity" (Isaiah 33:24).

In the meantime, in this earthly life, healing serves a special purpose: to be a concrete manifestation of the saving power and mercy of the

Lord; to make his divine love and forgiveness *real* for people. Think of how Jesus' healing of the paralyzed man lowered through the ceiling made real the deeper healing of forgiveness: "'That you may know that the Son of man has authority on earth to forgive sins'—he said to the paralytic—'I say to you, rise, take up your pallet and go home'" (Mark 2:10-11). The physical healing is proof of the spiritual healing. Think also of the leper, long cast away from society, and suffering the gradual rotting of his flesh, kneeling before Jesus and saying, "If you will, you can make me clean." Think of how the love of God must have been made powerfully real for him in the words of Jesus, "I do will it; be clean," resulting in immediate healing (Mark 1:40-41). Think again of Jesus' healing of the blind beggar Bartimaeus.

The key in these miraculous healings is the manifestation of the liberating kingdom of God. At the same time, they reveal the identity of the One who performs the healing: Jesus comes from God, and indeed is one with God—Divinity from Divinity. In the Gospel of John, for example, Jesus indicates that a purpose of his miraculous signs is to bear witness to his identity and origin: "If I do [the works of my Father], even though you do not believe me, believe the works, that you may know and understand that the Father is in me and I am in the Father" (John 10:37-39); and, "The works which the Father has granted me to accomplish, these very works which I am doing, bear me witness that the Father has sent me" (John 5:36).[18] The healings of the Apostles bore witness that they, too, were sent by God (see Acts 3–4). In manifesting the kingdom and revealing the identity of its messengers, healings are meant to elicit faith from those healed, and anyone else who might observe or learn about the healing.[19]

Redemptive Suffering and "Redemptive Healing"

Blessed are those who mourn, for they shall be comforted. . . . Blessed are those who are persecuted for righteousness' sake, for theirs is the kingdom of heaven.

—The Gospel According to Matthew 5:4, 10

The Lord Jesus . . . has sent me that you may regain your sight and be filled with the Holy Spirit.

—The Acts of the Apostles 9:17

Healings, then, reveal both a kingdom and a king. But as we saw in the healing of the blind Bartimaeus, this king rules from the cross. After his arrest, furthermore, the king makes clear to the earthly ruler Pontius Pilate that his kingdom and kingship are "not of this world" (John 18:36). *Physical healings, then, are not the whole gospel.* They are partial, incomplete—foretastes of the complete healing of heaven; foretastes meant to lead a person into a (deeper) relationship with the king and Divine Physician. Accordingly (and obviously), it is not true that everyone who comes to the Lord, without exception, is healed of their physical ailments. Moreover, of those that Jesus and the apostles healed or raised from the dead, many of them (presumably) got sick again, and all of them died. Christ, in fact, asks us to take up our crosses and follow him on his path of suffering (see Luke 9:23), just as he did with St. Paul, who three times begged to be healed of the "thorn in my flesh," receiving only this answer, "My grace is sufficient for you, for my power is made perfect in weakness" (2 Corinthians 12:9). Like St. Paul, in their flesh, disciples of Jesus Christ "complete what is lacking in Christ's afflictions for the sake of his body, that is, the church" (Colossians 1:24). This is what we often call "redemptive suffering."

None of this, however, is meant to diminish our belief in miraculous healing or make us believe that healings are meant to be extremely rare. The Lord is not sparing in his desire to heal—he is, in fact, quite liberal, as the Gospels show:

- He **healed all** who were sick. (Matthew 8:16, emphasis added)
- Jesus went about all the cities and villages . . . **healing every disease and every infirmity.** (Matthew 9:35, emphasis added)
- And **he healed many** who were sick with various diseases, and cast out many demons. (Mark 1:34, emphasis added)
- They ... brought to him **all** that were sick, and besought him that they might only touch the fringe of his garment; and **as many as touched it were made well.** (Matthew 14:35-36, emphasis added)
- **All** those who had any that were sick with various diseases brought them to him; and **he laid his hands on every one of them and healed them.** (Luke 4:40, emphasis added)
- The crowd sought to touch him, for power came forth from him and **healed them all.** (Luke 6:19, emphasis added)

And why wouldn't he be liberal with healings? Christ is the Son of God. He created us, redeemed us, and loves us. He is moved to compassion by our suffering (see Mark 1:41; Matthew 9:36). He came to give us abundant life (John 10:10). He came as the Divine Physician (see Matthew 9:12), a physician of soul and body: *he heals bodies to manifest his love, and to further his healing work of forgiving and redeeming souls.* It is for this reason that in addition to "redemptive suffering," we might perhaps also rightly speak of "redemptive healing."

Many Christians, of course, go too far in their expectation of physical healing and other temporal blessings, thinking that if these do not come, then there is necessarily something wrong with someone's faith. Yes, faith is an important factor (as we will see below), but as we know, in addition to God's will to heal there is also God's will for us to share in the cross of Christ. *For most of us Catholics, however, in the apparent "conflict" between redemptive suffering and redemptive healing, it is in all probability more likely that we go too far in the "redemptive suffering" direction.* We must remind ourselves that the same God who said, "Deny [yourself] and take up [your] cross daily and follow me" (Luke 9:23), also said, "The blind receive their sight and the lame walk, lepers are cleansed and the deaf hear" (Matthew 11:5), and "Whatever you ask in prayer, believe that you receive it, and you will" (Mark 11:24).

In the Gospels, Jesus never rebukes someone for asking for healing. If anything, he sometimes complains of a lack of faith, preventing the reception of what is asked. For example: "[The father of the child] said . . . 'If you can do anything, have pity on us and help us.' And Jesus said to him, 'If you can! All things are possible to him who believes'" (Mark 9:21-23). Again, this does not mean that every time prayer for healing is not answered, it is because there is not enough faith. Sometimes, the Lord's will for salvation requires that physical healing be delayed for the sake of spiritual strength and healing (see Romans 12:7-10). Yes, delayed: for all those who die in God's friendship will receive *complete* physical healing in the eternal life, whatever partial physical healings they may have received in time.

Do we believe in God's desire to heal? Do we have faith that the Lord can do deeds of healing for us, and through us?[20]

"Your Faith Has Made You Well"

"Ask, and it will be given you; seek, and you will find; knock, and it will be opened to you. For everyone who asks receives, and he who seeks finds, and to him who knocks it will be opened."

—The Gospel According to Matthew 7:7-8

"If you abide in me, and my words abide in you, ask whatever you will, and it shall be done for you."

—The Gospel According to John 15:7

Ask in faith, with no doubting, for he who doubts is like a wave of the sea that is driven and tossed by the wind. For that person must not suppose that a double-minded man, unstable in all his ways, will receive anything from the Lord.

—The Letter of James 1:6-7

This leads us to another important aspect of healing evident in the ministry of Christ: *faith*. It is through faith that God brings his salvation to the world. Likewise, when he sends out evangelists with the message of salvation through faith, it is also through faith that the miraculous feats of healing, which accompany the preaching, come about. The faith of the individual to be healed is often of critical importance. To a person whom he has just healed, Jesus frequently declares some variation of "Your faith has made you well" (see Mark 5:34, 10:52; Luke 17:19, 18:42; see also Matthew 8:13, 9:22, 29; Luke 7:50). Conversely, when Jesus encounters unbelief, little or no works of healing can be performed (see Matthew 13:53-58 and Mark 6:1-6).

While the faith of the sick person is important, faith can, in a sense, also be "borrowed." Recall the case of the paralytic in the second chapter of the Gospel of Mark. After the man is lowered through the roof, Jesus sees *the faith of the man's friends*; on that basis, he tells the paralytic that his sins are forgiven, and shortly after heals him (Mark 2:3-5, 10-12). This kind of sharing of faith also occurs with the Roman centurion whose servant is healed (see Matthew 8:5-13, Luke 7:1-10), the Canaanite woman whose daughter is healed (see Matthew 15:28), and the synagogue ruler whose daughter is raised from the dead (see Luke 8:49-55).

The faith of the minister of healing is also important. Occasioned at one time by his disciples' inability to drive out a demon, and at another time by his own ability to make a fig tree wither, Jesus teaches that faith has the ability to move mountains. "Nothing will be impossible to you," he says (Matthew 17:20). "If you have faith and never doubt

... whatever you ask in prayer, you will receive" (Matthew 21:21-22; see also Mark 11:21-24).[21]

Lastly, it is important to mention that while faith is of great importance for healing, it is not sufficient for salvation: "If I have all faith, so as to remove mountains, but have not love, I am nothing" (1 Corinthians 13:2).

Commissioned and Empowered by the Holy Spirit

Go into all the world and preach the gospel to the whole creation. . . . And these signs will accompany those who believe: in my name they will cast out demons; they will speak in new tongues; they will pick up serpents, and if they drink any deadly thing, it will not hurt them; they will lay their hands on the sick, and they will recover.

—The Gospel According to Mark 16:15, 17-18

After modeling it for them, Jesus commissioned his apostles and disciples to heal in their evangelization efforts.[22] When he sent them on mission, both during his ministry and after his resurrection, he almost always included miraculous signs of healing in the commissions he gave them. For example,

- He called the twelve together and gave them power and authority over all demons and **to cure diseases,** and he sent them out to preach the kingdom of God and **to heal.** (Luke 9:1-2, emphasis added)
- He called to him twelve disciples and gave them authority over unclean spirits, to cast them out, and **to heal every disease and infirmity.** . . . "Preach as you go, saying, 'The kingdom of heaven is at hand.' **Heal the sick,** raise the dead, cleanse lepers, cast out demons." (Matthew 10:1, 7-8, emphasis added)
- "Whenever you enter a town and they receive you . . . **heal the sick** in it and say to them, 'The kingdom of God has come near to you.'"[23] (Luke 10:8-9, emphasis added)

Authorized through these commissions and empowered by the Holy Spirit poured out upon them, the apostles and disciples abounded in healings, just as their Lord had. The Book of Acts, especially, makes this crystal clear: "Many wonders and signs were done through the apostles" (2:43; see 5:12). In the Gospel of Mark, we read: "[The apostles] went forth and preached everywhere, while the Lord worked with them and confirmed the message by the signs that attended it" (Mark 16:20). The Book of Acts also attributes miracles of healing specifically to Sts. Peter (see Acts 3:1-10; 5:15; 9:33-34, 40-41), Paul (see Acts 14:3, 8-10; 15:12; 19:11-12; 20:9-10; 28:8-9), Stephen (see Acts 6:8), and Philip (see Acts 8:6-7). St. Paul also refers to such signs in his letters, including the passage from 1 Corinthians with which we began our introductory chapter (2:1-5; see also Romans 15:18-19; 2 Corinthians 12:12; 1 Thessalonians 1:5).

In these examples, miraculous healing is specifically connected to the preaching of the gospel as a confirmation of its message and a manifestation of the kingdom of God having come near. It is found among missionaries and apostles. But there is another context for healing in the New Testament—seemingly unattached to the evangelization of unbelievers, but taking place in and among the faithful—for their building up in faith.

In speaking of the various spiritual gifts given the faithful to build up the body of Christ, St. Paul lists "gifts of healing" (1 Corinthians 12:9) and he lists "healers" among those God has appointed to serve the common good in the Church (12:28). In another letter, St. Paul mentions, in passing, that God "works miracles" among the faithful (Galatians 3:5). Jesus seems also to speak of miracles of healing not necessarily connected to the evangelization of unbelievers when he says, "These signs will accompany those who believe: . . . they will lay their hands on the sick, and they will recover" (Mark 16:17-18).

Why mention this in a discussion of healing in evangelization? For two reasons. First, it tells us that gifts of healing are not only meant for great evangelists like the apostles. They are also meant for the ordinary faithful. "These signs will accompany those who believe," Jesus says. "Those who believe" will manifest certain signs. In a certain sense, then, they are normal; we should expect that "these signs" be found among the faithful.

The second reason we mention gifts of healing among the faithful, which are not necessarily connected to evangelization, is that sometimes these gifts *are* so connected. Many of us are engaged in evangelization efforts among the baptized who have been previously evangelized to various, yet inadequate, degrees. A person with some measure of faith can have it deepened, strengthened, and enlivened by the experience of receiving or observing a healing. This is building up the body of Christ in the gospel of the kingdom of God. This too is evangelization.[24]

Extraordinary Signs of Healing in the Early Church

We have just briefly reviewed the scriptural basis for healing in evangelization and found that healing and other signs are essential adjuncts to evangelization. Healing and evangelization go together like the proverbial "two peas in a pod." But was this only meant for Jesus, the apostles, and the very early Church? What about *after* the New Testament era—after the age of the apostles? Were miraculous signs like healing present throughout the history of the Church?

Let's begin with the early centuries. According to the testimony of the Church Fathers, miraculous signs remained in the Church, in abundance, in the first centuries after the age of the apostles. When commenting on the Gospel of Mark chapter 16, verse 28, the great seventeenth-century Jesuit commentator Cornelius à Lapide goes so far as to say that it is clear from the writings of Church Fathers that almost all Christians in the early Church wrought miracles of one kind or another.[25] He cites St. Justin Martyr, Tertullian, and Lactantius of the second and third centuries. Other early writers also testify to the relative commonness of miracles among ordinary Christians, especially in the context of evangelization. These include St. Irenaeus of Lyon (second century),

Origen (third century), St. Cyprian of Carthage (third century), St. Cyril of Jerusalem (fourth century), and St. Hilary of Poitiers (fourth century), among others.

In the second century, St. Irenaeus wrote,

> Those who are in truth His disciples, receiving grace from Him, do in His name perform [miracles], so as to promote the welfare of other men, according to the gift which each one has received from Him. For some do certainly and truly drive out devils, so that those who have thus been cleansed from evil spirits frequently both believe, and join themselves to the Church. Others have foreknowledge of things to come: they see visions, and utter prophetic expressions. Others still, heal the sick by laying their hands upon them, and they are made whole. Yea, moreover, as I have said, the dead even have been raised up, and remained among us for many years. And what more shall I say? It is not possible to name the number of the gifts which the Church, throughout the whole world, has received from God . . . and which she exerts day by day for the benefit of the Gentiles, neither practicing deception upon any, nor taking any reward from them. For as she has received freely from God, freely also does she minister.[26]

St. Irenaeus, and the other Fathers listed, bear witness to miracles performed by ordinary Christians. Many saints performed miraculous healings and signs. These include Sts. Cosmas and Damian (third century), St. Martin of Tours (third century), St. Antony (third and fourth century); and especially missionary saints like St. Patrick (fifth century), St. Augustine of Canterbury (sixth century), and many more.

Of St. Martin of Tours, it is written,

> The gift of accomplishing cures was so largely possessed by Martin, that scarcely any sick person came to him for assistance without being at once restored to health. This will clearly appear from the following example. A certain girl at Treves was so completely prostrated by a terrible

paralysis that for a long time she had been quite unable to make use of her body for any purpose, and being, as it were, already dead, only the smallest breath of life seemed still to remain in her. . . . [Martin] cast himself down on the ground and prayed. Then gazing earnestly upon the ailing girl, he requests that oil should be given him. After he had received and blessed this, he poured the powerful sacred liquid into the mouth of the girl, and immediately her voice returned to her. Then gradually, through contact with him, her limbs began, one by one, to recover life, till, at last, in the presence of the people, she arose with firm steps.[27]

Between recognized saints and ordinary Christians, we have testimony of literally hundreds of healings from the age of the Fathers of the Church.[28]

And why not? The Son of God had come into the world to reveal the face of the Father. And upon returning to the Father, the Son had given his Church the Spirit that belongs both to the Father and the Son, so that the Church had truly become his body—his presence in the world. The Church would now do what he did, in his name and by his power.

A Decline

The witness to healings in the early Church is very significant. By the late fourth century, however, healings and other miracles seem to have had decreased to a point where figures such as St. Augustine and St. John Chrysostom declared that they had ceased—or at least that certain fuller manifestations had ceased.[29] They recognized that miracles occurred in great abundance in the early Church, but saw that things were not quite the same in their day. St. John Chrysostom said, "The present church is like a woman who has fallen from her former prosperous days."[30]

There are a number of theories for why miraculous signs, including healing, dwindled in number. Pope St. Gregory the Great thought that miracles increased during times when the Church especially needed them.[31] St. Thomas Aquinas similarly believed that miracles were necessary during the early Church to confirm the faith and spread it, and God willed to decrease the number of miracles as the Church became established so that the faith could spread by ordinary means such as preaching and teaching. Many others held a similar view.

Some commentators believe that miracles decreased for different reasons: lukewarmness and other faults of Christians, a decrease in expectant faith, a growing tendency to diminish the role of the laity, general cultural trends of devaluing the body (which we clearly see in the Manicheans and Gnostics, but also found expression among orthodox Catholics), and overreaction to the heretical charismatic movement known as Montanism.[32] We will not try to answer this question here. It is clear that, whatever the reasons, there was a decline of healings and miraculous signs in the Church, particularly among ordinary Christians.

As was pointed out, St. Augustine believed that the certain miraculous manifestations had ceased. But he didn't believe that all miracles had ceased. In fact, he kept records at the Shrine in Hippo of all the healings that occurred there.[33] Before his Baptism, furthermore, he himself had been healed—and it encouraged him greatly. In his autobiographical *Confessions*, he tells the story:

> I have not forgotten, nor shall I pass in silence, the bite of Your scourge and the wonderful swiftness of Your mercy. During those days you sent me the torture of toothache, and when it had grown so agonizing that I could not speak, it came into my heart to ask all my friends there present to pray for me to You, the God of every kind of health. I wrote this down on my tablet and gave it to them to read. As soon as we had gone on our knees in all simplicity, the pain went. . . . Thus in that depth I recognized the act of Your will, and I gave praise to Your name, rejoicing in faith.[34]

Another healing, told in his book *The City of God*, concerns a Christian woman of high standing named Innocentia who suffered from breast cancer. After praying, she received a dream in which she was told "to watch on the woman's side of the baptistery and ask the first newly-baptized woman who met her to sign the affected place with the sign of Christ. This she did; and she was immediately restored to health."[35]

These two stories are remarkable examples of healing achieved through the instrumentality of ordinary Christians. In the same chapter of *The City of God* where the story of Innocentia is told, St. Augustine tells many other stories of miraculous healings, most of them mediated through the relics of the saints and through the reception of the sacraments.

As the centuries moved on, despite any decline in frequency, the Church continued to experience many miraculous healings. As in St. Augustine's account, healings have often come through the relics and intercession of the saints, the sacraments, and at pilgrimage shrines. The waters at the shrine of Our Lady of Lourdes have brought countless healings, as have the pilgrimage shrines of St. Martin of Tours and of St. James of Compostella. Beatifications and canonizations in the Church have long been made only with confirmatory miracles, usually healings, through the intercession of the deceased saints. Many other healings are recorded especially as occurring in connection with great missionary and renewal movements. The Franciscan movement led to many healings, as did the renewal efforts of St. Vincent Ferrer and the evangelization efforts of missionaries like St. Francis Xavier.

St. Francis Xavier is a particularly interesting case of an evangelist—he is the patron of the missions with a "reputation for miracles" (*claritudo miraculorum*) of many kinds. During his life he is said to have healed many, including a beggar with ulcerous legs and a blind man whose sight he restored, as well as multiple people he raised from the dead.[36]

Many other saints are recorded as having healed others during their lives: St. Francis, St. Dominic, St. Bernard, St. Anthony of Padua, St. Paul of the Cross, St. Catherine of Siena, St. Teresa Margaret of the Sacred Heart, St. Francis of Paola, St. Martin De Porres, St. John Bosco, St. Pio of Pietrelcina, St. Andre Bessette, St. Frances Xavier Cabrini, Blessed Solanus Casey, and many more. Truly, miraculous healings have had a continual presence in the Church.

Performative Speech

Let's recall two quotes cited earlier. The first is of Pope Emeritus Benedict XVI: "The *evangelium*, the Gospel, is not just informative speech, but performative speech—not just the imparting of information, but action, efficacious power that enters into the world to save and transform."[37] The second, which we quoted in the introductory chapter, is from St. Paul: "My speech and my message were not in plausible words of wisdom, but **in demonstration of the Spirit and power,** that your faith might not rest in the wisdom of men but in the power of God" (1 Corinthians 2:4-5, emphasis added).

The gospel is not just a matter of words, but of power—the power of God. This power comes in various forms, but we have seen that the testimony of the Sacred Scriptures, and the history of the Church thoroughly confirm that among these, miraculous physical healings are prominent. Our Blessed Lord Jesus Christ, fulfilling the Old Testament prophesies of the Messiah and the Messianic Age, performed countless healings in his ministry and taught that his disciples would perform greater works than he (see John 14:12). The apostles and disciples of Christ carried on the work of healing, and the early Church, for centuries, received such gifts not just through great saints but also through ordinary Christians. Even when there seemed to have been a decline in miraculous healings, they never disappeared in the Church, but continued to occur throughout her history.

In the next chapter, we will consider whether God desires gifts of healing to be exercised in the Church today for the spreading of the gospel, and what the modern Magisterium has said about these phenomena.

Chapter 2

HEALING TODAY AND
THE MODERN MAGISTERIUM

Healings are signs of [Christ's] messianic mission (cf. Lk 7:20-23). They manifest the victory of the kingdom of God over every kind of evil, and become the symbol of the restoration to health of the whole human person, body and soul. They serve to demonstrate that Jesus has the power to forgive sins (cf. Mk 2:1-12); they are signs of the salvific goods, as is the healing of the paralytic of Bethesda (cf. Jn 5:2-9, 19-21) and the man born blind (cf. Jn 9).

—Congregation for the Doctrine of the Faith,
Instruction on Prayers for Healing, 2001, 9.

In a solemn tone, Tim read the prayer on the back of the card: "Jesus . . . I consecrate myself . . ."

Twenty minutes earlier, Tim had said, "I am not a Christian, though I'm not totally closed off to it."

Ten minutes before that, Tim and Steve were seated next to each other at the barber shop, getting haircuts. Steve overheard the barber ask, "So how have you been doing?" and Tim's answer: "I've still got lots of pain."

Steve wondered whether he ought to reach out to the man, to pray for whatever physical condition he was dealing with. He was busy, having important things to do. But he figured that if their haircuts ended around the same time, then that would be enough of a sign that God wanted it. And lo and behold, that is exactly what happened!

"Hi there! I have a gift for you!" Steve gave Tim a miraculous medal. "I overheard you say that you have chronic pain, and I wanted to talk to you because I often pray for people to be healed of physical conditions, through Jesus Christ, and sometimes Jesus answers by healing them. Are you a Christian?"

They went to a private place to pray. Tim had back problems and severe nerve pain in his back, neck, shoulder, and leg. The pain in his leg was an eight out of ten.

After leading him through prayers of forgiveness of those who had hurt him, Steve led Tim through a prayer of repentance for sin. Then they prayed for healing of the body, and shortly thereafter, the pain was gone—completely gone.

"I can't believe this! I can't believe this!" Tim kept saying.

As if it were not already clear to him from the prayer, Steve proclaimed to Tim that it was Jesus Christ, risen from the dead, who was healing him, and that he could take the first step: to consecrate his life to Christ. That's when Tim solemnly read through the consecration prayer on the back of the card.

Α ✝ Ω

If this story does not convince you that the Lord wants us to include prayers for healing in our evangelization efforts today, then . . . *keep reading.*

Think of it this way: Would Tim have likely consented to give his life over to Jesus Christ, Our Blessed Lord, if Steve had approached him without offering him hope of physical healing from the Lord? *Perhaps.* Indeed, Tim had said that though he was not a Christian, he was open to it. . . . *Then again*, he said this *after* having been given some hope of miraculous healing.

In truth, however, the desire for healing from illness and other physical conditions leads by a very natural logic to consideration of the gospel of Jesus Christ and its claims, to life in the Church, and to hope in eternal life. We saw this in the previous chapter, when we considered the ministry of Jesus, the apostles, and early Church history.

The Magisterium (teaching authority) of the Church confirms this. In the 2000 *Instruction on Prayers for Healing*, the Vatican Congregation for the Doctrine of the Faith wrote, "Presuming the acceptance of

God's will, the sick person's desire for healing is both good and deeply human, especially when it takes the form of a trusting prayer addressed to God"; and that it is "praiseworthy for individual members of the faithful to ask for healing for themselves and for others."[38] *The human desire for deliverance from disability and illness is normal, natural, and within God's plan.*[39] With this being the case, it is no wonder that in the Sacred Scriptures we discover that healing from disability and illness has a special connection with the fulfillment of God's promises in Christ. "Healings," as the above-mentioned Vatican instruction says, "are signs of [Christ's] messianic mission . . . signs of the salvific goods."[40] In other words, for example, the healing of physical deafness or blindness can point us to the healing of spiritual deafness or blindness; the healing of physical illness or disability can point us to deliverance from spiritual illness or disability. Healings point us forward in hope of the bodily resurrection, and serve as concrete, personal revelations of the love of God.

Having examined the role of healing in evangelization in the Sacred Scriptures and the history of the Church, we now move on to consider *the role of healing in evangelization today.* Does God want to use miraculous signs, like healing, to confirm and spread the faith at this juncture in history? After all that we have seen in the Scriptures and Church history, it may seem like the obvious and emphatic answer is "yes." But let's not jump to conclusions! Recall that although healings and other miraculous signs have never departed from the Church, there was a very long period in which they seem to have declined. And considering the possibility that they may have declined not by the fault of man but by the will of God, we see that it is not at all immediately obvious, based on the Scriptures and Church history alone, that the Lord now wants them to increase.

It will be helpful for us to consider, therefore, the "signs of the times" (Matthew 16:3). To do this, we will examine some of the social and cultural trends that characterize our time. While we do this, we will continue, as needed, to draw from the Scriptures and Church Tradition, for in every age they are normative for us as Catholics. But we will focus in a special way upon the Magisterium of the Catholic Church, for it is the authority of Christ himself, given by him to the Church, to interpret Scripture and Tradition in each generation. The Magisterium has been given "the duty of scrutinizing the signs of the times and of interpreting them in the light of the Gospel."[41] As it turns out, moreover, in the past six or so decades, the Magisterium has said much that relates to the topic of healing in evangelization.

The Signs of the Times: Rejection of God

Let us begin by considering the signs of the times. Most of us within the Church have probably heard the terms culture of death, secularism, and relativism used in reference to our age, especially in Western civilization. We may also have heard the terms materialism, consumerism, nihilism, modernism, postmodernism, and maybe even post-Christian. Within these terms are captured many facets of a profound and growing intellectual, cultural, moral, social, and spiritual disorder. Most of us are aware of it: human life and dignity is degraded by the spread of abortion, euthanasia, illicit reproductive technologies, population control, pornography, human trafficking, racism, pollution, war, and poverty. The natural bonds of family are attacked by divorce, contraception, and the redefining of marriage. The natural complementarity of the sexes is denied, and one's biological sex is turned into a matter of choice. Solidarity and brotherhood are dissolved as differences of opinion become the grounds for profound animosity, with one group wrathfully pitted against another. Beyond being simply distinguished and separate from the state, faith and religion are made separate from everyday life and are increasingly driven out of the public square. And in many cases, these evils are tolerated or even positively promoted by those in positions of power in government, media, and business.

There's more: we fill our lives with consumer goods, entertainment, and technology, leaving little room for what is truly valuable. We seek a feeling of connection through social media but are left largely disconnected from one another. As narcissists, we pursue wealth, power, freedom, and personal fulfillment while the poor and needy suffer just outside the door. As activists, we chase human progress while failing to love, honor, and worship God our Creator. And we find ourselves lonely, empty, broken, and addicted.

Finally, these disorders infect even the members of the Church, who, as a result, often seem to have lost their identity, unsure even that the Son of God has come in the flesh, cleansed the Church, formed her into his body, revealed himself to her in the Scriptures and Tradition, given her his Spirit, and invested her with his divine authority.

At its core, we find that this manifold disorder reflects a profound turning away from God, the Creator, for the sake of things in the world that he created. Without God, humanity has lost its bearings, no longer understanding the things that are in the world (to which they are so attached), let alone the things of heaven. And the result, figuratively and literally, is war:

> What causes wars, and what causes fightings among you? Is it not your passions that are at war in your members? You desire and do not have; so you kill. And you covet and cannot obtain; so you fight and wage war. You do not have, because you do not ask. You ask and do not receive, because you ask wrongly, to spend it on your passions. Unfaithful creatures! Do you not know that friendship with the world is enmity with God? Therefore whoever wishes to be a friend of the world makes himself an enemy of God. (James 4:1-4)

In this Scripture passage from the Letter of James, notice how "friendship with the world," where the passions and desires dominate life, is *the same* as being the enemy of God. They are two sides to the same coin. Notice also that this friendship-of-the-world-which-is-enmity-with-God leads to animosity toward other people. We see the same dynamic in the Garden of Eden, in the fall and its aftermath. Adam and Eve made themselves "friends of the world" by stepping out of the order established by God in favor of their desire for the forbidden fruit which they deemed "good for food, . . . a delight to the eyes, and . . . [able] to make one wise" (Genesis 3:6). They became, thereby, enemies of God, for immediately afterwards they found it necessary to "[hide] themselves from the presence of the Lord God" (Genesis 3:8). They also became wounded in their relationship with one another—when confronted with his actions, Adam blamed Eve for what he had done, revealing the break in their relationship (see Genesis 3:9-12). This wounded relationship between human beings quickly finds expression in all-out murder when one of their sons, Cain, takes the life of his brother Abel (see Genesis 4:1–16).

It is this dynamic which we see repeated in the world today. Following our unruly passions and desires, we find ourselves estranged from God, estranged from one another and, even more, estranged from ourselves.

But this is nothing new, is it? We've already identified this dynamic in the letter of the Apostle James, originally written to a first-century Christian audience, and in the first parents of the human race. How is today different from any other time? *Is* it different?

Before we answer this question, a note of caution: we shouldn't try to compare the evils of one age with the evils of another in a spirit that writes people off as hopeless, or refuses to love them where they're at.[42] That being said, there is undeniably something different about our age, something that cannot be said about any other time: *we live in a "post-Christian" age.* Western society and culture is in an advanced stage of degradation after having rejected Christianity and with it the God of Jesus Christ, both of which it had at one time embraced. We knew God, and have rejected him! If the disorder that we see today appears to us greater than in previous ages, then it seems that this would be the reason.[43]

We, as a culture, en masse, have rejected God. In many ways, we are similar to the great cultures of the ancient world, including Rome: without knowledge of God, advanced in worldly accomplishments, puffed up in pride, filled with disorders. But ancient Rome had not at one time known Christ and then later rejected him. Western culture has. This is the *most important* sign of the times that can be identified.

Having identified it, what does it tell us? Our society's rejection of God is, in fact, the great sign of the times that inspires the work of the Saint Paul Evangelization Institute. As we often say, "Society has turned its back on God! The culture is dying! Souls are being lost!" This is the great evil of our time that summons us to battle: to greater faithfulness, prayer, sacrifice, and evangelization. Christians are always called to evangelize, but in our age the task of evangelization takes on a special urgency.

Furthermore, there are a number of positive aspects of the situation that should spur us on all the more. In an encyclical on the "urgency of missionary activity," Pope St. John Paul II wrote,

> Our own times offer the Church new opportunities. . . . We have witnessed the collapse of oppressive ideologies and political systems; the opening of frontiers and the formation of a more united world due to an increase in communications; the affirmation among peoples of the gospel values which Jesus made incarnate in his own life (peace, justice, brotherhood, concern for the needy); and a kind of soulless economic and technical development which only stimulates the search for the truth about God, about man and about the meaning of life itself.[44]

Indeed, as he says, there are great opportunities for evangelization. The failure of godless systems leaves openings for godly ways of life. The rapid development of technology brings opportunity as well as dangers. Reaction against evils creates openness to good. Emptiness, woundedness, and meaninglessness can lead to openness to God. In a certain sense, the world is ripe for conversion. In the same encyclical quoted above, St. John Paul II famously wrote, "I sense that the moment has come to commit all of the Church's energies to a new evangelization. . . . No believer in Christ, no institution of the Church can avoid this supreme duty: to proclaim Christ to all peoples."[45]

So the culture has turned its back on God, but there are signs of hope; and we need to evangelize using all of our energies. . . . What does any of this have to do with healing in evangelization? The answer is this: having rejected God *so emphatically*, our society has made itself in special need of all divine means of spreading the gospel. We can no longer simply teach and proclaim the truths that have been handed down to us in the Church, for the rejection of those truths are built into the very culture. Although there are reasons for hope in the fresh proclamation of the gospel, it may not be enough to counter the profound disorder and rejection of God we see today. Could signs and wonders also figure into the picture?

The Signs of the Times: Postmodernism and Extraordinary Deeds

Perhaps an answer to this question can be found in a more specific, already mentioned sign of the times: our society is postmodern. Now it is not important for us to make a full analysis of the complex phenomenon of postmodernism;[46] it suffices to list a few general characteristics. Postmodern society tends to reject reason, authority, absolute truth, and "metanarratives" (overarching stories that give meaning to all of life). And obviously, the Christian faith values reason, submits to divine authority, proclaims absolute truths, and offers a specific metanarrative in the life, death, resurrection, ascension, and second coming of Jesus Christ.

This poses a huge problem. Things we have to offer—important, essential things—are the very things they don't want. We will most certainly fail, on the whole, to *persuade* the postmodern man of the truth of Christianity. But remember the quote from St. Paul with which we began the first chapter of this training? We don't only have truth to offer—we also have power:

When I came to you, brethren, . . . my speech and my message were not in plausible words of wisdom, but in demonstration of the Spirit and of power, that your faith might not rest in the wisdom of men but in the power of God. (1 Corinthians 2:1-5)

Our patron, St. Paul, did not rely so much on the arguments of human reason, but allowed God to confirm his words with extraordinary deeds. To the postmodern man, who says, "There's *my* truth, and there's *your* truth," a tangible experience is immensely better than merely a good argument.

But it's more than just postmodern man. Whatever time or culture you are in, man remains a combination of soul *and* body—spirit *and* flesh—and so God reveals himself in both word *and* deed. At the Second Vatican Council, the bishops of the Catholic Church emphasized it this way:

This plan of revelation is realized by deeds and words having an inner unity: the deeds wrought by God in the history of salvation manifest and confirm the teaching and realities signified by the words, while the words proclaim the deeds and clarify the mystery contained in them.[47]

St. Paul says as much:

I will not venture to speak of anything except what Christ has wrought through me to win obedience from the Gentiles, by word and deed, by the power of signs and wonders, by the power of the Holy Spirit. (Romans 15:18-19)

Jesus Christ did not come to argue, but to reveal. He preached with words, and demonstrated the words with works. From miraculous works like the dividing of the Red Sea through Moses (see Exodus 14), the raising of the widow's son by Elijah (see 1 Kings 17), and the multiplication of the loaves or the healing of the man born blind by Jesus (see John 6 and 9), to loving works like St. Francis of Assisi embracing a leper, Blessed Pier Giorgio serving the poor of Turin, and St. Teresa of Calcutta pulling a dying man with rotten flesh from the gutter—as in all of these, *deeds must go with words*; and the more extraordinary the deeds (the more grace-filled, the more out-of-this-world, the more expressive of love they are), the more likely they will be to shake some sense into postmodern man.

The Signs of the Times: Pluralism and Commercialism

There are two other signs of the times to consider. First, we live in a pluralistic society: in general (notwithstanding a particular aversion to Christianity), people see various religions and ways of life as being more or less equal. Likewise (notwithstanding a certain hypocrisy), there is a strong distaste for making judgments between differing viewpoints—a profound indifferentism. Whether it is between Christianity and other worldviews/religions, or between Catholicism and non-Catholic Christian denominations, the "I'm good; you're good" attitude makes it hard to make convincing the unique claims of the Catholic Church.

The second is that our society is "commercialistic": in the market of goods and the market of ideas, we are constantly being bombarded with products to buy and ideologies to buy into. From the supermarket, the department store, and online stores, we are given an infinite set of buying choices, each product vying for our attentions and our wallets. From veganism to animal rights, to organic and non-GMO food, to gender-theory, to theories of race-relations, to transhumanism, to pro- and anti-vaccination movements, to the pro-choice movement, to the opposing positions on climate change, etc., we are given viewpoints (right or wrong) on myriads of specific issues, all vying to become our single overarching moral concern.

Though some of these things are good, others bad, and others neutral, none of them are worthy of our total devotion. Many people give their lives over to these ideologies, or even to consumer products, as if they were the most important things in the world. We once had someone on the street confidently tell us that his god was the fashion designer Versace. He had no interest in hearing about Christ.

With the great many products, lifestyles, worldviews, and religions to choose from, each being treated as a matter of indifference on the one hand, or aggressively marketed to us or embraced with single-hearted devotion on the other, the gospel of Jesus Christ can seem like merely one choice among thousands of options. What can possibly make it stand out in the crowd? Shall we give up on proclaiming the uniqueness of the gospel and give in to pluralism? Or should we employ modern marketing strategies to make it more palatable to the tastes of the consumer, giving in to commercialism?

Neither of these paths are options for us. In either, we make ourselves unfaithful to Christ. So what can possibly make the gospel stand out in the crowd? A rhetorical question: How many of the purveyors of these products, ideologies, and religions are curing the blind, driving out demons, and raising the dead?

The Magisterium and Charisms of the Holy Spirit

Jesus . . . makes [his disciples] share in his ministry of compassion and healing . . . The Holy Spirit gives to some a special charism of healing so as to make manifest the power of the grace of the risen Lord.
—*Catechism of the Catholic Church*, 1506–1508

Let's recap. We came to three conclusions. First, our culture is deeply estranged from God, so we need all the means we can muster to bring souls to him and to effectively evangelize in the world today. Second, in all times the gospel can only be effectively proclaimed by words *with corresponding deeds*; but because of the postmodern context of our culture, we need these powerful deeds to support our words *all the more*. Third, with so many choices of worldview, religion, way of life, and so many products marketed to us, we need to stand out distinctly among thousands of options. Each one of these three conclusions, drawn from the signs of the times, suggest that miraculous signs like healing may be an important part of what we need for our evangelization efforts to be effective in our world today. *They suggest that perhaps we ought to beg the Lord for this gift.*

But these further conclusions, in turn, might lose much of their force if the Magisterium of the Catholic Church didn't also provide us strong supports for it. Are miraculous signs, like healing, still to be found? Are they meant to confirm the gospel? Can ordinary Christians expect ever to be used as instruments of the Lord's healing for others when evangelizing?

First, let's consider the topic of miraculous signs as extraordinary gifts of the Holy Spirit. St. Paul addresses the topic of the charisms most thoroughly in 1 Corinthians chapters 12 through 14. In chapter 12, he lists extraordinary gifts such as the working of miracles and healing together with more ordinary gifts such as faith and wisdom. The Magisterium of the Catholic Church, during her long history, has likewise not artificially separated the extraordinary gifts from the ordinary ones.

The Catholic Church is "continuationist," rather than "cessationist." What does that mean? Cessationism is the belief that the signs and wonders of the New Testament Church—the extraordinary spiritual gifts (charisms) like tongues, prophecy, or healing—were only intended for a time and ceased to be present in the Church after that period of time had elapsed. Continuationism, on the other hand, is the belief that the signs and wonders of the early Church have continued. Historically, cessationism had a particular connection to Protestantism, which largely denied the validity of the miracles of Catholic saints and miracles received through the sacraments, pilgrimages, and sacramentals like blessed medals and relics. They also often saw the cessation of extraordinary spiritual gifts as implied in the doctrine of *sola Scriptura*. This has partially changed, however, in modern times, which has seen great growth in continuationism among Protestants, together with healings and other signs. The Catholic Church, for her part, has never been fully cessationist,[48] but being faithful to Sacred Scripture, and having witnessed miraculous signs continuously in her history, she sees these signs as *a means of confirming divine revelation* (even condemning as anathema those who deny it).[49]

Ordinary Christians, Extraordinary Gifts

What about ordinary Christians? Can they be used by the Lord as means of healing? We can say that after its first few centuries, there was in the Church a stronger emphasis on healing through the sacraments, relics, the intercession of the saints, and through particularly holy Christians, usually religious. There was much less of a sense—though it was not absolutely excluded—that the ordinary Christian could be an instrument of the Spirit of God in this way.[50]

However, the Second Vatican Council set the stage for a retrieval of the ancient tradition of ordinary Christians making use of the extraordinary charisms. Specifically, the Council's teachings on the universal call to holiness and to mission (arguably its most important accomplishment) made clear what may not have consistently been clear: lay Christians are called to the heights of holiness, and each is given a true share in the mission of the Church.

The Fathers of the Second Vatican Council teach: "All the faithful of Christ of whatever rank or status, are called to the fullness of the Christian life and to the perfection of charity."[51]

They also teach that "the Christian vocation by its very nature is also a vocation to the apostolate. No part of the structure of a living body is merely passive but has a share in the functions as well as life of the body: so, too, in the body of Christ, which is the Church."[52]

Further, the Council teaches that each member of the Church is endowed with charismatic gifts to assist them in carrying out their share of the Church's mission:[53]

For the exercise of this apostolate, the Holy Spirit Who sanctifies the people of God through ministry and the sacraments gives the faithful special gifts also (cf. 1 Cor. 12:7), "allotting them to everyone according as He wills" (1 Cor. 12:11) in order that individuals, administering grace to others just as they have received it, may also be "good stewards of the manifold grace of God" (1 Peter 4:10), to build up the whole body in charity (cf. Eph. 4:16). From the acceptance of these charisms, including those which are more elementary, there arise for each believer the right and duty to use them in the Church and in the world for the good of men and the building up of the Church, in the freedom of the Holy Spirit who "breathes where He wills" (John 3:8). This should be done by the laity in communion with their brothers in Christ, especially with their pastors who must make a judgment about the true nature and proper use of these gifts not to extinguish the Spirit but to test all things and hold for what is good (cf. 1 Thess. 5:12, 19, 21).[54]

Also,

It is not only through the sacraments and the ministries of the Church that the Holy Spirit sanctifies and leads the people of God and enriches it with virtues, but, "allotting his gifts to everyone according as He wills," He distributes special graces among the faithful of every rank. By these gifts He makes them fit and ready to undertake the various tasks and offices which contribute toward the renewal and building up of the Church, according to the words of the Apostle: "The manifestation of the Spirit is given to everyone for profit." These charisms, whether they be the more outstanding or the more simple and widely diffused, are to be received with thanksgiving and consolation for they are perfectly suited to and useful for the needs of the Church.[55]

Notice in the above quotes that the charisms are gifts given to individuals to build up the body of Christ. They are not limited to clergy or religious, but rather the Holy Spirit "distributes [these] special graces among the faithful of every rank."

Speaking specifically of the charism of healing in 2001, the Vatican Congregation of the Doctrine of the Faith wrote along the same lines:

The "charism of healing" is not attributable to a specific class of faithful. It is quite clear that St. Paul, when referring to various charisms in

1 Corinthians 12, does not attribute the gift of "charisms of healing" to a particular group, whether apostles, prophets, teachers, those who govern, or any other.[56]

The Importance of the Extraordinary Charisms

Let's pull out another three points from the long Second Vatican Council quotes given above. First, the charisms they speak of include both "the more outstanding [and] the more simple and widely diffused." They clearly include extraordinary gifts like healing and miraculous signs.

Second, we see that charisms—while surely inferior—are parallel and complementary to the sacraments: "It is not only through the sacraments and the ministries of the Church that the Holy Spirit sanctifies and leads the people of God and enriches it with virtues . . ." Building upon this teaching, Pope St. John Paul II taught that "there is no conflict or opposition in the Church between the institutional dimension and the charismatic dimension. . . . Both are co-essential to the divine constitution of the Church founded by Jesus, because they both help to make the mystery of Christ and his saving work present in the world."[57]

Third, we see that the charisms "are to be received with thanksgiving and consolation for they are perfectly suited to and useful for the needs of the Church." In other words, the Magisterium highly values these charisms and encourages us to be open to them and to accept them. In a speech in 1998, St. John Paul II said, "Today, I would like to cry out to all of you gathered here in St. Peter's Square and to all Christians: open yourselves docilely to the gifts of the Spirit! Accept gratefully and obediently the charisms which the Spirit never ceases to bestow on us!"[58] In 2016, the Vatican Congregation for the Doctrine of the Faith wrote, "The authentic charisms, therefore, come to be considered as gifts of indispensable importance for the life and mission of the Church."[59] All of this is in accord with the teaching of St. Paul, who tells us to "earnestly desire the spiritual gifts" (1 Corinthians 14:1; see also 12:31).

Seeking the Extraordinary Charisms

So the charisms are important, and we should be open to them. But should we seek them? Should we pray for them? The Second Vatican Council's Dogmatic Constitution on the Church, *Lumen Gentium*, states that "extraordinary gifts are not to be rashly sought after."[60]

If they ought not to be sought after rashly, the implication seems to be that they may be sought after without rashness. We will discuss this topic at more length in chapter 4, Praying for the Gifts.[61] It is also important to note that the passage from *Lumen Gentium* on seeking extraordinary gifts continues by saying that the Church has the special competence of overseeing and discerning the validity and proper use of such gifts, which means that they should be exercised in peace and communion with our priests and bishops, with docility and obedience.[62]

So we ask again: should we seek for the gift of healing for use in our evangelization efforts? Once more, it seems that we should. In Scripture, we have a striking model of praying for these gifts for the purposes of evangelization. In the Acts of the Apostles, chapter 4, Sts. Peter and John are being examined by the Sanhedrin for preaching Christ and healing a cripple. After they are admonished and released, they offer prayers of thanksgiving to God and, with others, continue praying like this: "enable your servants to speak your word with all boldness, as you stretch forth [your] hand to heal, and signs and wonders are done through the name of your holy servant Jesus" (4:29-30 NAB). When they had completed their prayer, "the place where they were gathered shook, and they were all filled with the holy Spirit and continued to speak the word of God with boldness" (4:31 NAB).[63]

So we have a biblical example of the apostles and others praying for signs and wonders to confirm the proclamation of the gospel, an example in which the prayers were answered. *We can also do the same.* If we do it without rashness, and recognizing the authority of the bishops, we can pray for the Lord to grant us, through his Spirit, gifts of healing for evangelization.

Signs, Manifestations, and Proofs of the Gospel

Let's look back at the quote from the Vatican Congregation for the Doctrine of the Faith, with which we opened this chapter:

> Healings are signs of [Christ's] messianic mission (cf. Lk 7:20–23). They manifest the victory of the kingdom of God over every kind of evil, and become the symbol of the restoration to health of the whole human person, body and soul. They serve to demonstrate that Jesus has the power to forgive sins (cf. Mk 2:1–12); they are signs of the salvific goods, as is the healing of the paralytic of Bethesda (cf. Jn 5:2–9, 19–21) and the man born blind (cf. Jn 9).[64]

The Magisterium of the Catholic Church confirms what the Sacred Scriptures and the history of the Church show us—that gifts of healing are useful for evangelization. And we know, in our times especially, that we need all the help that we can get. Many of us who spend time doing public evangelization have seen hostility to the gospel; but even more, we've seen great indifference to it. We've seen the quasi-universalism, the belief that almost everyone will end up in heaven, even without repentance. We've seen the attitude that says, with calm self-assurance, "Nah, I'm good!" We see all these things, and we console ourselves with the thought that we are "planting seeds." Now, don't take this wrongly—nobody's conversion happens all at once and in an instant; many times, "planting seeds" is the only thing we can do, and the most appropriate thing we can do.

Even so, we may have forgotten that in Jesus' parables about the kingdom of God, the analogy of planting seeds is about more than just the gospel taking time to grow. It is about how the seed of the gospel is often devoured, scorched, choked, and prevented from bearing fruit because the soil it is being planted on is *bad soil*. We must consider the possibility that the message of the gospel is often rejected because the soil of the culture is *bad soil*. For today, it seems like we need something more than good moral and intellectual formation in the faith. We need more than good arguments. We need the power of God to bear witness to the truth of what we are preaching. Miracles like healing can only happen through God's power and as such they can be potent means to fertilize the bad soil. By the very nature of a miracle, God's power and presence are shown forth without much room for doubt. And then God's divine revelation and the salvation he offers in Jesus Christ is shown forth forcefully, in ways suited to the condition of those without faith. Faith is stirred up by these external proofs of the gospel.

A ✝ Ω

Does God want to use miraculous signs of healing today to confirm and spread the faith? *By now it should be pretty easy to answer in the affirmative.*

Once, in a sermon, St. Augustine wrote, "Let no one, brethren, say that our Lord Jesus Christ does not do those things now, and on this account, prefer the former to the present age of the Church."[65]

We would do well to heed his words: *we should not think that the Lord does not do those things now.* As we've seen, the Church, in her teaching office, has consistently affirmed the legitimacy of these extraordinary gifts of the Holy Spirit today. And indeed they are already occurring in the Church and in our apostolate.

In the next chapter, we will go over a four-step model for praying for healing.

Chapter 3

FOUR-STEP PRAYER MODEL

Steve asked me what the problem was, and I told him that I was suffering from shingles. Then he told me to touch the area where the disease was, and I touched my chest, although my whole left breast was covered with them, and was aching so much. He started the prayer for healing, and then asked me if the pain was still there, or if it had gone away any. I touched the rashes on my body to see whether or not I could feel the irritation the clothes caused me in the affected area. I could feel almost no pain, and I also did not feel the rashes except the drying, wounded areas, and I answered that eighty percent of the pain had gone. He prayed again, and after that there was no itching, no irritation, and no pain. I only felt the hard scars of the wounded parts that seemed to have miraculously dried up. Shortly after we adjourned, I ran inside my room to remove my religious habit and see if what I felt was really true. When I looked, I noticed my shingles had withered. I saw only the withered tips of the wounds caused by the shingles. . . . I was very tired from the trip [when I arrived home in Nairobi], but very thankful, since the rashes and itching caused by the shingles never came again.

—Testimony of Sr. Christine, from the Sisters of the
Sacred Heart of Jesus, on her experience of being healed at a
St. Paul Evangelization Institute retreat in Bloomington, Indiana

In this chapter, we are going to teach a simple and straightforward method of praying with people for healing—most especially for physical illnesses, injuries, and disabilities.[66] This model is flexible, able to be used in different settings such as street evangelization, prayer groups at your parish church, or even public places (like the grocery store) when you're out running errands or spending time with family and friends. Although our method has four basic steps, it is based on a common method which numbers the steps at five.[67] *Depending on the situation, some steps may be specially emphasized, de-emphasized, or even skipped altogether.* Be flexible and let the Holy Spirit guide you as you learn and grow as an effective instrument of God for healing. Let's get right into it.

Step One: Interview and Preparation for Prayer

This first step has two main parts. First, in the preliminary interview we ask questions to help us discern what the person needs prayer for and how we should pray for that need.[68] Second, in the preparation we prepare the person for prayer by explaining to them the process, telling them a faith-building story or two, and perhaps dealing with one or more of a few common blocks that can prevent healing.

The amount of time we have with the person and the circumstances will determine the length of time we spend on each of these. In some cases, especially when we are praying for random people out on the street or in a grocery store, the entire process may take less than thirty seconds. When we know the person and have more time, this step may take five to ten minutes, or even longer. *In all cases, we are prudent and wise, and we let the Holy Spirit lead us; we are flexible as we keep an eye on how the person we are praying for responds during the process.* Let's look more closely at this first, two-part step.

Part One—Preliminary Interview

Begin by finding out about the condition the person suffers from. Be friendly and compassionate as you ask questions. It is not necessary to identify every single problem or detail, however. God knows what is wrong, and even if you don't get all the relevant information in this first step, you will have another chance later on, during the "reinterview" step. A short summary of the condition is usually enough to get started. Begin by getting the person's name and ask them some basic questions, such as:

- What would you like prayer for today?
- How long have you had this condition?
- Do you know what caused it? What was happening in your life when it started?
- Does this run in your family?
- Have you seen a doctor? What did the doctor say?
- Did anything significant or traumatic happen to you around the time this condition developed, or a few months prior? (You may need to explain this question—see Appendix A, Extra Topics: Forgiveness and Repentance.)
- Have you forgiven the person that caused this injury? (You may need to explain this question—see Appendix A, Extra Topics: Forgiveness and Repentance.)
- Could this condition be related to anything you have done in the past? (If it seems that this could be the case; you may need to explain—see Appendix A, Extra Topics: Forgiveness and Repentance.)
- Is there some movement or activity that causes you pain? On a scale from one to ten, how much pain are you in right now?
- Do you believe that Jesus Christ can heal you?

Pay attention to the person's words, emotional state, and overall demeanor as you ask questions and listen to their answers, and be open to the promptings of the Holy Spirit. These questions are important; they will enable you to pray to the specific condition[69] and can help you determine if there are other conditions of an emotional or spiritual nature like fear, anger, hatred, unforgiveness, self-rejection, serious sin, or some other spiritual attachment. Sometimes these can become blockages to healing, and so you will probably want to pray for them to be removed as well, and/or address them in some other way such as compassionate conversation, encouragement, well-placed and welcome advice, etc.[70]

Part Two—Preparation Building Faith

Once you have a basic handle on what the problem is, and depending on the situation and how much time you have, you may want to tell a story or two about people who have been healed either through your own prayer or through others in our apostolate. If you only have a few seconds you might say something like,

> Let's pray for this condition. I know that God can heal you. I'm part of an organization that has people who pray for healing, and we've seen many miracles. One man who we prayed for had cancer and was confined to a wheelchair for seven years. After one of our teams prayed for him he got up and walked. Later his doctor confirmed that his cancer went into remission. Another time a woman with a birth defect was healed. She had one leg two inches shorter than the other. After prayer both legs were even. Shortly afterwards she got doctor verification which confirmed that both of her legs were the same length!

It can be hard for some people to tell others about how God has used them to heal, as if it were prideful bragging. Remember that we don't tell these stories to build ourselves up, but to give glory to God and build faith in the person we are ministering to. Just make sure to give the glory to God when you tell such stories. It is God who provides the faith which the person may need to receive healing.

Explanation of the Prayer Process

At this point, **it is usually helpful to briefly explain to the person what they might expect from the prayer.** Explain that sometimes a person gets healed immediately after a quick prayer, and sometimes a healing comes gradually and is complete only after praying several times. You can tell them that you will usually keep praying as long as they are experiencing the presence of God, or as long as there is progress, such as the reduction of pain. You might explain that you usually place a hand on the person's shoulder or, if it is appropriate to do so, on the location of the illness or injury.[71]

You should also ask the person to let you know if at any time they are experiencing the presence of God or sensing anything in their body. It often happens that the area that God is going to heal will get warm, start tingling, or experience a feeling of electricity as soon as you begin praying; but not always. You want to know if the person is having any of these sensations because it can help you know where God wants you to focus your prayers.

Sometimes the person will want to pray to God for their healing at the same time as you are praying; but this is usually counter-productive. **Tell the person not to pray, but just to relax, close their eyes, receive the prayer, and to pay attention to what God is doing with their body.**

If they have not already told you of something in the preliminary interview, and if it is appropriate to the situation, you may also tell them at this time that it can be useful to pray a prayer of forgiveness and/or repentance prior to praying for healing.[72]

If this suggestion quickly brings a person or situation to their mind, or if they had already told you something about the need for forgiveness or repentance earlier in the preliminary interview, you can lead them in prayers to address these at this time, just prior to praying for the condition itself.

Lead them in the ways indicated below or in similar ways. They neither necessarily need to share the details with you, nor do they even need to pray the following prayers out loud; they can pray in their mind so that the Lord alone can hear them.

—[Have them bring to mind the person they need to forgive; another person, or even themselves.]

—"In the name of Jesus, I forgive _____ for _____."

—[Have them bring to mind their sin, especially serious sins, and those that may have some relation to the condition.]

—"I repent of the sin of _____. I renounce and reject it. I am sorry for offending you; God, please forgive me!"

Step Two: Healing Prayer

This second step has two main parts. **First, calling upon the Holy Spirit; second, praying for healing.** We will begin, however, by making some initial comments on peripheral points like demeanor, posture, voice, etc.

So what about your demeanor? *You should cultivate compassion for the suffering person, and your demeanor should be one befitting that inner attitude.* Be attentive and kind, reflecting the Lord's goodness. Don't put on a front or show; be genuine.

What about posture? Our Lord said that his disciples would lay hands on the sick and that they would be healed (see Mark 16:18). There is something special about physical touch that can dispose us to effectively give and receive the gifts of God, and most people instinctively recognize this. Others, however, feel uncomfortable being touched, especially by a stranger. For this reason, as mentioned above, *you should usually ask the person if you can place your hand on their shoulder or on the location of the illness or injury.* Use common sense, and be open to the Holy Spirit's guidance; depending on the circumstances, you may not even want to ask. One of our evangelists, for example, sensed strong discomfort in a person, and so opted to stand and pray about two feet away from them, and she still experienced a healing. In such cases, you can pray with hands folded or in the "orans" posture.[73] You should never lay your hands in a place which is inappropriate, which usually limits you to the shoulder, the arms, the legs below the knee, the feet, the neck, the head, and the upper back.[74] In the Sacred Scriptures we see healing take place both with and without the laying on of hands.

When you pray, it is usually best to keep your eyes open, so that you can be attentive to how the person is doing; there may be some indication of what God is doing in them, for example, a peaceful smile, tears, strong emotion, or even a disturbance of some kind. That indication, in turn, may lead you to ask questions that will help you get to the root of the problem, giving greater insight on how to pray.

What about voice? Use your normal tone of voice, and know that it is OK to pray silently at times. If you normally spend some time praying silently, during the preparation step let the person know that you will be doing this, so that they will not feel awkward or unsure.

Part One—Calling Upon the Holy Spirit

When beginning your prayer, first call upon the Holy Spirit, and have expectant faith that he will come. You can simply say "Come Holy Spirit."

Or you can pray something a bit lengthier such as "Lord, we ask you to send your Holy Spirit upon Bob. Send your healing presence to be with us. Come Holy Spirit!"

You may also choose to briefly invoke the Blessed Virgin, saints, and the holy angels to intercede and protect.

After calling on the Holy Spirit, **wait for a period of time** to see if the Holy Spirit is making his presence known in a discernable way within you, and within the person you're praying for. The waiting can take as long as thirty seconds or more, provided that you have the time and have let the person know that this is what you will do.

Then **ask the person if they are sensing anything**—usually heat, tingling, electricity, or an overwhelming feeling of peace—and if so, you should vocally thank God for what he is doing, and ask for more.[75] If the feelings are focused on some area of the body, it may be good at that point to focus your prayers there and ask God to heal that area, laying your hands there if appropriate. Sometimes a quick prayer is all you need at this point, and the person is healed.[76]

If the person is not experiencing the presence of God in any tangible way, you can let them know that it's OK. Many times people who are healed experience some special feeling or sensation, but many other times people don't. At one of our past trainings, a woman named Lydia believed that she would be healed and was eagerly waiting and expecting to feel heat, tingling, or some other sign, but she never did. However, she was healed one-hundred percent!

Either way, whether they experience something or not, you should proceed to pray specifically for healing at this point.

Part Two—Praying for Healing

When praying for healing, there are two types of prayer that you can make use of. The first type is a **prayer of petition**. This is where you appeal to God for healing. You may say something like "Lord, in the name of Jesus, I ask you please to heal Betty's cancer. Strengthen her immune system and help her regain the strength that she has lost through chemotherapy."

Or, "Heavenly Father, I beg you, in the name of Jesus, to heal James of his back injury. Come with your healing power and restore his bulging disks to health. Strengthen the muscles, bring the bones into proper alignment, and remove all pain, in the name of Jesus Christ your Son."

Or, "Lord Jesus, I ask you to heal Geoff of anxiety and depression. Come to him and remove any fears that may be preventing him from serving you with the joy and peace of the Holy Spirit. Fill him with the knowledge of your profound love for him. I ask this in your most holy name, the name of Jesus."

The second type of prayer is the prayer of authority, or prayer of command. In Catholic theology, the prayer of command is closely associated with the concept of "adjuration,"[77] where some help or action is urged on the strength of something holy, such as the name of God.

Most miracles performed in the New Testament follow prayers of command. As Christians, we have authority in Jesus' name and can at times command demons, the human body, sickness, and disease.[78] When engaging in prayer of command, always make the prayer "in the name of Jesus" and speak directly to the condition itself. At times you may need to command a "spirit of affliction"[79] or the specific disease to leave, in the name of Jesus. You can say something like, "Pain, be gone now, in the name of Jesus. I command you: ligaments, bones, tendons, and cartilage of the back to be healed now, in Jesus' name. Inflammation, leave right now. Swelling, go down."

Or, "In the name of Jesus Christ, I command and adjure your respiratory system to return to full health and proper functioning. Lungs open; breathe freely, without restriction."

Or, "Headache, be healed now, in Jesus' name. I adjure any spirit of affliction to leave John, in the name of Jesus Christ."

Note the difference between the prayer of petition and the prayer of command. The first is directed to God, and the second is directed at the disease or condition, or even at a demonic spirit (a spirit of affliction or illness, a particular disease, etc.).[80] The first primarily reflects the Christian's childlike reliance and trust upon God, and the second primarily reflects the Christian's mature assumption of God-given authority. How should we choose between the two? How should we begin our prayer and how should we continue? Pray on it. Rely on the Holy Spirit's guidance.[81] You may choose, out of humility and a sense that your faith is not strong enough, to use the prayer of petition exclusively until such time as you receive a clear direction to make use of the prayer of command. On the other hand, you may be inspired to step out in faith and use mostly the prayer of command. You may use one or the other; begin with one, and then move on to the other; or use both together. Sometimes it makes sense to begin with prayers of petition, and if no progress is being made, to switch to prayers of command and see if anything changes.

In either case, pray with confidence and expectancy. Trust in the power and mercy of God. Also, try to be as specific as possible and pray into the symptoms, as well as the root cause of the issue, as you saw in the examples above. Here is another example:

Lord, we thank you for your healing presence. We ask you to heal Joe's back injury from the fall that he took last year. Remove the pain and restore movement. In the name of Jesus, we ask for healing of the verte-brae, cartilage, tendons, ligaments, bones, muscles, tissues, and anything else that may have been damaged in the fall. Remove the anxiety that he has been experiencing since the accident. Back be healed, in Jesus' name! Come Holy Spirit!

Step Three: Reinterview

This third step involves gathering more information to determine how to continue. **After a short time of praying, stop and check to see if anything has happened during prayer.** If a condition can be tested to see if there is any improvement, now is the time to do it.[82] Improvement, or the lack thereof, lets you know what the Lord is doing, and hence how to proceed—how to continue praying, how long to continue praying, etc. Partial healings can also increase faith, leading to more healing. Ask the person to try to do something that they couldn't do before, like walk without crutches, run (if safe), or move their arm in a certain way. Ask if the pain is gone or has decreased in any way. Oftentimes healing will come gradually, and it may take three or four brief prayers before the affliction is completely healed.

In the Gospel of Mark, for example, Jesus prays over a blind man and then "reinterviews" him, asking, "Do you see anything?" (8:23). The man answers, "I see men; but they look like trees, walking" (8:24). Jesus prays a second time, and the man is completely healed (see 8:25).

Another example of progressive healing, quoted at the beginning of this chapter, comes from one of our retreats: Sister Christine was healed gradually of painful, itching shingles. She testified,

He started the prayer of healing, and asked me if the pain was still there, or if it had gone away any. I touched the rashes on my body to see whether I could feel the irritation the clothes caused me in the affected area. I could feel almost no pain, and I also did not feel the rashes much except the drying, wounded areas, and I answered that eighty percent of the pain had gone. He prayed again, and after that I felt that there was no irritation, no itching, and no pain.

This kind of occurrence is not uncommon. So if there is any improvement at all, make sure to thank and praise God for the improvement, and pray again. Where possible, continue to pray for the person as long as there is improvement taking place.

If the person feels heat, tingling, electricity, or some other unusual sensation, it may mean that the Lord is healing them. Continue praying until it subsides. If that feeling is in a particular area of the body, focus your prayers there and continue, until the feeling subsides. If the feeling moves to another spot, refocus your prayers there.

If the condition is not able to be tested right away for improvement and there is no heat, tingling, or other unexpected sensation, and if it is appropriate, reinterview by exploring potentially undiscussed obstacles of unrepentance and unforgiveness. If these exist, you can lead the person in repentance and forgiveness and pray again. If you are not reinterviewing, and it is possible, just pray for a longer period of time. Do these things with prudence and following the inspiration of the Holy Spirit.

If you have prayed and nothing at all seems to be happening, do pray again, but be open to the Holy Spirit leading you to try a different approach. See if there is anything else about the condition or the circumstances surrounding it which was not mentioned before. Return to some of the questions in the preliminary interview stage, especially if they were not asked at that time. Perhaps there is need for the person to forgive someone (including themselves) or repent of some sin. Perhaps there is a spirit of affliction that should be commanded to leave in Jesus' name. Again, be attentive and open to the promptings of the Holy Spirit and follow his lead.

Sometimes it will seem like there may be a blockage to healing that goes beyond straightforward cases of unrepented sin or unforgiveness. Sometimes especially strong or complex emotions, acknowledged or unacknowledged, intervene—emotions such as anger, fear, hopelessness, self-condemnation, unworthiness, etc. Sometimes there are demonic obstacles—some kind of demonic oppression or obsession that hinders healing. While we can pray for the healing of emotions and against demonic influence in simple ways,[83] in many of these cases the person requires more involved prayer of inner healing or deliverance which you're not able to offer. In still other times, the person may need professional counseling, psychotherapy, or even exorcism. It is important to be able to recognize when you are getting out of your depth, and when appropriate, to be able to refer the person or ask them if they have considered professional help.

Usually, if no progress is being made, it is a good practice to pray three times, reinterviewing after each, before quitting. In one of his letters, St. Paul says that he prayed three times for an affliction to be taken from him and then he received a word from the Lord, leading him to resign himself to the fact that God wanted him to suffer this affliction for a time (see 2 Corinthians 12:7-10). Depending upon the situation and the relationship you have with the person, you may decide to pray with them again at a different time.

If a person is not healed, don't worry. Tell them that it is often the case that a person will either be healed overnight or the condition will improve over the next few weeks. Tell the person also to trust God and pray often, saying something like,

> You can continue praying for healing! And you know, we can be sure that if it will be the best for your soul and for the kingdom of God that you be healed, God will heal you. We can also be certain that if you stay faithful to God until the end, you will be healed: either in this life or in the next!

One Saint Paul Street Evangelization (SPSE) evangelist prayed for a woman who had an irreversible condition called thrombosis. She was not healed when he prayed for her, though she felt like she would be healed. When she woke up the next day she was one-hundred percent healed, and she contacted the evangelist to let him know.

Another time, the same evangelist prayed for a woman who had a rare and irreversible condition in her intestines. She had had fourteen surgeries and had been told that there was nothing else that could be done for her. She expected that she would soon die from the condition. The evangelist prayed for her, and no healing occurred. But the woman felt deeply touched by the experience and was certain that God had sent the evangelist to her reveal his love for her. She clutched her new miraculous medal as they parted ways that day.

We find that most people we pray for end up very thankful that we cared enough to go out of our way to pray for them. They can see our compassion for them. The goal of praying for healing is that the person feels loved and, with most people, that goal will be achieved simply by praying for them with sympathy and kindness, whether or not they are actually healed of a condition.

Step Four: Post-Prayer Proclamation and Recommendations

This fourth step has two main parts. First, proclaim the gospel in some fashion, speaking the truth to them in love. Second, give post-prayer recommendations, encouragement, and offer a final prayer. Be flexible on how these steps are carried out, as the needs of the situation demand.

Part One—Proclamation of Gospel and Speaking the Truth in Love

If a person is healed, they usually become extremely open to the message of the gospel. If they are not healed, they still may be open to the gospel. **If they are not a Christian, tell them that Jesus Christ is the Lord, and he is alive; and if they were healed, tell them that it was Jesus that healed them.** Ask them what they know about Jesus. Tell them, if necessary, that Jesus Christ, the Son of God, came to earth to restore us to fellowship with God and asks us to repent of our sinful deeds. He loves us and has compassion on us in our weakness, but will come again to judge every human being according to their response to his grace, and what they have done. Or tell them that God is real, that he created them and loves them, and desires to be in union with them now and in eternity. He is all-good and hates evil, and in Jesus he provides a way of life through which he conquers evil in us and in others. Depending on how they respond, ask if they are willing to take the first step to becoming a Christian by committing their life to Jesus right then and there. Be prepared to help them make such an act, with the help of a prayer of consecration to Jesus, or some other means.

Praise God's goodness in front of the person. Tell something of your own testimony. It may be important to lead them to repentance as well and, if they are not already doing so, to help them to start walking with God. God will use a healing to bring a person to repentance and conversion, so we should act right away to help start that process. SPSE's "One Good Reason" method is often appropriate here.

Be straightforward and genuine. Don't be preachy. Be attentive to the person and what is most needed, and let the Holy Spirit give you what to say. Be bold.

Part Two—Recommendations and Final Prayer

There are important recommendations to make at this time, some of which were mentioned previously. One relates to "losing" a healing. The devil will, in fact, sometimes try to scare a person and "steal" a healing, if the condition had something to do with him. So **if a person is healed, tell them that they can take authority over their healing in Jesus Christ if the condition or pain starts to come back.** They can command it to leave in the name of Jesus.[84]

Nancy, for example, was healed of an arm injury during one of our trainings. During post-prayer recommendations, she was told not to let Satan rob her of the healing, and if the pain or restricted mobility came back, to rebuke him, saying "Get behind me, Satan!" Lo and behold, the pain came back later that night and, unafraid, Nancy rebuked the devil, and the pain went away again.

Tell the person not to discontinue their medication, even if it seems like they are healed, especially if the condition is something that can't be observed easily. Let the doctor help them make those kinds of decisions. If possible recommend the person follow up with you after having conferred with the doctor and/or tested the condition in everyday life to confirm or test for a healing.

Other recommendations might relate to their life in Christ in the following days, weeks, and months. Encouragement, advice, and promises of prayer may be appropriate. If they were not healed, encourage them to continue praying for their healing regularly—that it sometimes takes time. Encourage them to draw near to God, and to pray daily. Exchange contact information, invite them to a church service or Bible study or to RCIA, or make plans to follow up with them for tea or coffee. In a nutshell: help them to take a step nearer to God, and then offer to walk with them on the continuing journey.

Lastly, it can be great to say a final prayer, asking the Holy Spirit to come into the person's life in a powerful way. The prayer can be something like,

> Come Holy Spirit! Fill John with your love, your peace, your joy and your wisdom. Refresh him in mind and body. Guide him into all truth. Make him a light to the nations and give him the strength that he needs to overcome the temptations of this world. Give him the grace to become a great saint in the kingdom of God!

In making this prayer, follow the lead of the Holy Spirit here, and recall what you have learned about the person so far. After a prayer like this, it is not uncommon for the person to be deeply touched by the presence of the Holy Spirit.

Praised be Jesus Christ! In the next chapter, we will address the question of praying for the gift of healing.

Chapter 4

PRAYING FOR THE GIFTS

While staying with [the apostles after his resurrection, Jesus] charged them not to depart from Jerusalem, but to wait for the promise of the Father, which, he said, "you heard from me, for John baptized with water, but before many days you shall be baptized with the Holy Spirit."
. . . **"You shall receive power when the Holy Spirit has come upon you; and you shall be my witnesses** in Jerusalem and in all Judea and Samaria and to the end of the earth."
—The Acts of the Apostles 1:4-5, 8 (emphasis added)

Here in the first chapter of the Acts of the Apostles, we see that by the command of the Risen Lord, the apostles, after the ascension, were to keep prayerful vigil, waiting for "the promise of the Father," the Holy Spirit. Filling them, the Holy Spirit would give them "power"; only then were they to go out and proclaim the gospel to the ends of the earth.

Then, as recounted in the Acts 2, the Holy Spirit came with gifts of boldness and with signs and wonders on the Feast of Pentecost.

For our part, we have received the outpouring of the Holy Spirit for witnessing to the gospel, and accompanying spiritual gifts, through the sacraments—Baptism and Confirmation especially. The *Catechism* teaches,

The Most Holy Trinity gives the baptized . . . the power to live and act under the prompting of the Holy Spirit through the gifts of the Holy Spirit. . . .

Baptism gives a share in the common priesthood of all believers. . . .

"Reborn as sons of God, [the baptized] must profess before men the faith they have received from God through the Church" and participate in the apostolic and missionary activity of the People of God. . . .

The effect of the Sacrament of Confirmation is the special outpouring of the Holy Spirit as once granted to the apostles on the day of Pentecost. . . .

[Confirmation] increases the gifts of the Holy Spirit in us; . . . it gives us a special strength of the Holy Spirit to spread and defend the faith by word and action as true witnesses of Christ, to confess the name of Christ boldly, and never to be ashamed of the Cross. . . .

[Confirmation] perfects the common priesthood of the faithful, received in Baptism, and "the confirmed person receives the power to profess faith in Christ publicly and as it were officially (*quasi ex officio*)."[85]

In previous chapters, we provided a scriptural, historical, and magisterial basis for healing in evangelization, and then explained a four-step approach to healing prayer. Before we begin to put this four-step model into practice, we ought to call upon the Lord to fill us with the Holy Spirit, renewing the graces we received in the sacraments. We ought to pray for an increase of faith, hope, and charity along with the special charism of healing so that miraculous signs will accompany our proclamation of the gospel. In this chapter, we will give some important background explanation for why we should do this, and instruction on just how to do it.

Rekindle the Gift of God That Is within You

I am reminded of your sincere faith. . . . Hence I remind you to rekindle the gift of God that is within you through the laying on of my hands; for God did not give us a spirit of timidity but **a spirit of power** and love and self-control. Do not be ashamed then of testifying to our Lord.

—The Second Letter of St. Paul to Timothy 1:5-8 (emphasis added)

In these words of St. Paul to St. Timothy, we learn that the grace of the sacraments (in this case the sacrament of Holy Orders) can be stirred up, rekindled, or renewed. Before we go out and exercise gifts of the Holy Spirit like healing, we ought to pray for these gifts and for all of the graces and virtues needed to exercise them fruitfully (especially knowledge, discernment, etc.). We need to stir up and renew the graces of the sacraments.

We also see this necessity illustrated powerfully in chapter 4 of the Acts of the Apostles, where we find the apostles and disciples praying for boldness and extraordinary gifts of the Holy Spirit, after having already received these gifts in abundance at Pentecost. In response to this prayer, in what has been called "the Pentecost of Renewal," they were filled with the Holy Spirit *for a second time, after Pentecost*, with extraordinary signs accompanying the event as before.

Let's consider what happened with the apostles more closely. Accompanied by great signs and wonders, the apostles proclaimed Jesus Christ after the event of Pentecost. At that time, as recorded in Acts 3, Peter and John had healed a man who had been lame from birth, giving them the occasion to proclaim the gospel just outside of the Temple. In chapter 4, the account continues:

> As they were speaking to the people, the priests and the captain of the temple and the Sadducees . . . arrested them and put them in custody . . . They called them and charged them not to speak or teach at all in the name of Jesus. . . . And when they had further threatened them, they let them go, finding no way to punish them, because of the people. . . . When they were released they went to their friends and reported what the chief priests and the elders had said to them. And when they heard it, they lifted their voices together to God and said, "Sovereign Lord, who didst make the heaven and the earth and the sea and everything in them, . . . truly in this city there were gathered together against thy holy servant Jesus, whom thou didst anoint, both Herod and Pontius Pilate, with the Gentiles and the peoples of Israel, to do whatever thy hand and thy plan had predestined to take place. **And now, Lord, look upon their threats, and grant to thy servants to speak thy word with all boldness, while thou stretchest out thy hand to heal, and signs and wonders are performed through the name of thy holy servant Jesus."**
>
> **And when they had prayed, the place in which they were gathered together was shaken; and they were all filled with the Holy Spirit and spoke the word of God with boldness. . . .**

With great power the apostles gave their testimony to the resurrection of the Lord Jesus, and great grace was upon them all. . . .

Now many signs and wonders were done among the people by the hands of the apostles. (Acts 4:1, 3, 18, 21, 23-24, 27-31, 33; 5:12, emphasis added)

What an account! Here we have a repetition, of sorts, of Pentecost: gathered in prayer, the disciples are filled with the Holy Spirit amid extraordinary signs. Afterward they preached the gospel powerfully and boldly, with accompanying signs. Clearly, it seems, the disciples received a renewal, rekindling, or stirring up of the special grace acquired earlier at Pentecost.

This renewal serves as a pattern for our own renewal. When we were baptized and confirmed, we received, like the disciples present at Pentecost, an outpouring of the Holy Spirit, including a share in charisms. Now, like the same disciples, we can ask God for a renewal.

There are many reasons why someone may need a renewal. The renewal the disciples sought in Acts 4 was in response to persecution. After having proclaimed Christ and healed a crippled man, Peter and John experienced pushback: they were arrested by the Sanhedrin, imprisoned, interrogated, and admonished. In praying then for a rekindling of the gifts of God once received, the disciples were doubling down on their evangelistic efforts—in accordance with what they said to the Sanhedrin: "Whether it is right in the sight of God to listen to you rather than to God, you must judge; for we cannot but speak of what we have seen and heard" (Acts 4:19-20). They were pushing back on the pushback. *What are other reasons we might want to stir up the sacramental graces we've received previously?*

One reason is that we may have had less than desirable dispositions at the time we received a sacrament. The *Catechism* teaches on the one hand that the sacraments communicate grace *ex opere operato* (by the very fact of the action's being performed), and on the other hand that *their fruits "depend on the disposition of the one who receives them."*[86]

Speaking about Baptism, St. Thomas Aquinas gives several reasons why the sacraments may not at once bear more fruit: inadequate repentance, lack of faith, lack of adequate preparation and devotion, inadequate response, sins, etc.—when these hindrances are removed, the fuller grace of the sacraments can be released.[87]

Another reason we have for stirring up the sacramental graces we've received previously is connected simply to the nature of the gifts and the laws of spiritual growth. What is accomplished in Baptism and Confirmation can be activated, deepened, strengthened, and/or matured. We can receive new gifts and charisms, and actuate or develop the ones we already possess. Some of the Fathers of the Church speak of these realities. Tertullian, for example, exhorts those to be baptized to pray for charisms right after coming out of the baptismal font.[88] St. Hilary of Poitiers wrote,

> We who have been reborn through the sacrament of baptism . . . receive [various gifts, including] the gifts of healing. . . . These gifts enter us like a gentle rain, and once having done so, little by little bring forth fruit in abundance. . . . When this gentle rain falls, the earth rejoices. But the rains are multiplied so that [at first] there are small streams; the streams then become raging waters, so that they become mighty rivers.[89]

Often gifts received will grow as we grow in holiness.

Whether we are renewing gifts already exercised, removing obstacles to gifts we should have received but didn't, or stirring up new gifts, we should be praying, with a spirit of humility and conformity to the will of God, for the Holy Spirit and for charisms and all the other spiritual gifts and virtues needed to exercise them effectively.

Earnestly Desire the Spiritual Gifts

Ask, and it will be given you; seek, and you will find; knock, and it will be opened to you. . . . If you then, who are evil, know how to give good gifts to your children, how much more will the heavenly Father give the Holy Spirit to those who ask him!

—The Gospel According to Luke 11:9, 13

Grace was given to each of us according to the measure of Christ's gift . . . for the equipment of the saints, for the work of ministry, for the building up of the body of Christ, until we all attain to . . . mature manhood, to the measure of the stature of the fullness of Christ.

—The Letter of St. Paul to the Ephesians 4:7, 12-13

Among the many gifts given to us, or made possible, through the sacraments we've received, are the charisms of the Holy Spirit like the gift of healing. In his First Letter to the Corinthians, St. Paul spends a good deal of space discussing the charisms. In that letter, particularly chapters 12 through 14, he makes their purpose and place in the Christian life clear: they are gifts dispensed to the faithful by the Holy Spirit as he wills, for the good of the Church. Charisms are not the most important gifts—the most important are gifts of a very different kind, the virtues of faith, hope, and charity, given to all at Baptism. Even so, charisms are good gifts meant to be put at the service of the body of Christ. They are referred to as "varieties of gifts," "varieties of service," "varieties of working," and "manifestations of the Spirit." In addition to gifts of healing, there are charisms like the utterance of wisdom or knowledge, teaching, faith, working of miracles, prophecy, tongues, discernment, etc. Again, they exist not so much for the benefit of the one performing them, but for the benefit of the Church. Thus, they must not be valued for their own sakes, nor made into symbols of status; but rather should be exercised in an orderly manner, and subject to apostolic authority and the virtue of charity.[90]

St. Paul twice exhorts the faithful in Corinth to "earnestly desire the . . . gifts," especially the greatest ones, which build up the body of Christ the most (1 Corinthians 12:31; 14:1; see 14:12). In case there is any doubt that Paul is referring to the charisms listed in 1 Corinthians 12, this is how Scripture commentator Cornelius à Lapide reads him, following St. John Chrysostom. When commenting upon this, à Lapide suggests that by prayer we should strive to obtain these gifts—like tongues, prophecy, healing, and so forth; but with pure motives, "not from any desire for superiority over others . . . but out of charity, that they may profit others and the Church at large by means of those gifts."[91] We may seek these gifts, we may pray for them; but only from the desire to serve, to build up the body of Christ.[92]

The Second Vatican Council's Dogmatic Constitution on the Church, *Lumen Gentium*, clarifies the matter further when it teaches, as we mentioned in chapter 2, that "extraordinary gifts are not to be rashly sought after."[93] Though we may seek these gifts, it must be without rashness; that is, only after careful consideration of the consequences, and of our motives, spiritual and moral maturity, and condition of life. Do we want the charism of healing in order to satisfy a prideful desire for attention, superiority, or praise? Have we not yet built a strong spiritual life or overcome habitual grave sin? How and where will we make use of the charism, and will its exercise negatively impact our ability to fulfill the responsibilities of our state in life?

For us who strive to be evangelists, this exhortation of St. Paul to "earnestly desire" the charisms takes on a special meaning. We, in a particular way, may be called upon to pray for charisms—for our very purpose is to build up the Church by helping to incorporate new members into her ranks. Furthermore, we should expect extraordinary charisms like healing to be manifest more abundantly when used in the work of evangelization rather than exclusively among churched individuals who have already come to Christ. These gifts, serving as signs to confirm the message of the gospel, are most appropriate in the context of evangelization, and God seems to grant them more often in those contexts.

If you are properly disposed, then, and you wish to make use of the four-step healing prayer model, it is important that you first spend some time in prayer for the charism of healing, and for supporting gifts and virtues like boldness, wisdom, and discernment. We, like the apostles and disciples in Acts 4, are constantly in need of the Lord's grace and help for everything we do. The graces we received once in Baptism and Confirmation can grow, like small saplings into mature plants—or, like a fire, become stirred up after having died down. We should take some quality time to pray for the Holy Spirit and his gifts. Our God is particularly generous in this matter: "If you then, who are evil, know how to give good gifts to your children, how much more will the heavenly Father give the Holy Spirit to those who ask him!" (Luke 11:13). As always, the effectiveness of prayer is increased when it is accompanied by fasting and works of charity (such as almsgiving), in a spirit of humility and obedience.

In addition to engaging in personal prayer for the Holy Spirit and his gifts, you may also choose to seek out others to pray with you—virtuous, mature Catholics, especially priests and deacons and others that already exercise the gift of healing. In various ways, our fathers and brothers, sisters and mothers in Christ can be instruments of God to "impart" spiritual gifts to us (see Romans 1:11), stirring up the graces we have received in the sacraments. Request others to pray with you, for you, or over you, to ask that the Lord fill you with the Holy Spirit and grant you a share in the gift of healing and other charisms.

First and foremost, we suggest this because "if two of you agree on earth about anything they ask, it will be done for them by my Father in heaven. For where two or three are gathered in my name, there am I in the midst of them" (Matthew 18:19-20). We also suggest this because those exercising a gift in the body of Christ may often be the very people whom God uses as instruments to impart that gift to others. We see these kinds of things in the Sacred Scriptures, where a share of the Holy Spirit, with spiritual gifts or manifestations of one kind or another, are sometimes "transferred" to some people through the agency of others. Many times, the probable or certain context is one of the sacraments or their Old Testament equivalents;[94] at other times, however, the context seems different.[95] In Acts 10:34-44, for example, a household of people are filled with the Holy Spirit at the mere preaching of St. Peter.

In 2 Kings 2:9-15, Elisha obtains a "double portion" of the Spirit from the prophet Elijah through his mantle, receiving the same miraculous gifts he had. We also see this in the history of the Church, where spiritual goods are continually shared among the faithful in heaven and on earth. Reflecting Elisha's request of Elijah, St. Thérèse asked "all the saints in heaven to obtain for her a double portion of their love," love with which, in turn, she would bear great fruit.[96] St. Francis Xavier, also, who taught little children to heal the sick he could not get to,[97] passed his gift to them in some way, presumably through prayer.

It is important to note that the charism of healing, like other charisms, is something that, if truly desired, should be desired "earnestly." It is often no good to give up after asking the Lord for a charism five, six, seven, ten, fifteen, or even thirty times. God does much work in us through our desires, and desires are proven through prayer and action done with perseverance. So if you truly desire the charism of healing, and you are properly disposed, pray for it continually, without losing heart. If the Lord doesn't want you to pray for it anymore, he will make it clear to you.[98] You also could begin to pray for people for healing, in simple ways, with humility and perseverance, making use of the four-step method. Even if it becomes clear that you don't have a charism for healing, you need not completely stop praying for people! Any Christian, whether with special charism or not, can pray for people for healing and expect that, at least from time to time, God will answer their prayer. This is especially true for the evangelist, for whom (all other things being equal) God will more often grant such signs, in confirmation of the message.

I Will Show You a Still More Excellent Way

Be transformed by the renewal of your mind, that you may prove what is the will of God, what is good and acceptable and perfect.
—The Letter of St. Paul to the Romans 12:2

After you have prayed with a pure heart for charisms, and have received them, you are now called to exercise them for the building up of the body of Christ. However, discernment must continue! The exhortation of the Fathers of the Second Vatican Council to not rashly seek after extraordinary gifts applies also to their exercise—*you must be vigilant in maintaining and increasing purity of heart as you put your gifts into practice*. A teacher for us in this task is St. John of the Cross.

In *The Ascent of Mount Carmel*, St. John teaches that those who have received charismatic gifts ought to purify from themselves all inordinate attachment and vain joy regarding them. When this is not done, there is danger of harming the faith of others, of vainglory or vanity, and of greatly hindering "discernment of the true gifts from the false and knowledge of how and at what time they may be exercised."[99]

Regarding this last point—the "how and at what time"—he teaches further:

> It is true that when God bestows these gifts and graces he gives light for them and an impulse as to the time and manner of their exercise. Yet souls can err seriously, . . . not using them with the perfection desired by God, at the time and in the manner he desires . . . [but] by some imperfect passion that was clothed in joy and esteem for these works. When this imperfection is not present, such persons decide to perform these works when and in the manner that God moves them to do so; until then they should not work them.[100]

St. John of the Cross's teaching here is characteristically very cautious about anything that can be a hindrance to love of God. "Love is not perfect if it is not strong and discreet in purifying joy with respect to all things, centering it only on doing God's will."[101] The exercise of spiritual gifts like miraculous healing occasions much joy, but the saint rejoices in exercising this gift only in the time and manner willed by God. *This demands that the one who exercises these gifts remains united to God through prayer, so to purify his heart and discern the time and manner for the exercise of the gifts.* Being "transformed by the renewal of [his] mind, . . . [he] may prove what is the will of God, what is good and acceptable and perfect" (Romans 12:2). This approach—the "more excellent way" of love of God and neighbor—imitates Jesus, who did nothing but what he saw the Father doing (see John 5:19-20). It will bear the most fruit for salvation of self and others.

Come Holy Spirit!

Come Holy Spirit, fill the hearts of your faithful and kindle in them the fire of your love. Send forth your Spirit and they shall be created. And You shall renew the face of the earth.

—Come Holy Spirit prayer

Come Holy Spirit! In all of the above matters, the Third Person of the Blessed Trinity, the Holy Spirit, is the essential companion for the evangelist. He pours the love of God into our hearts, equips us to share the gospel, and prepares the hearts of our hearers. In his encyclical on evangelization, Pope Blessed Paul VI wrote,

> Evangelization will never be possible without the action of the Holy Spirit. . . . It is the Holy Spirit who, today just as at the beginning of the Church, acts in every evangelizer who allows himself to be possessed and led by Him. The Holy Spirit places on his lips the words which he could not find by himself, and at the same time the Holy Spirit predisposes the soul of the hearer to be open and receptive to the Good News and to the kingdom being proclaimed.

Techniques of evangelization are good, but even the most advanced ones could not replace the gentle action of the Spirit. The most perfect preparation of the evangelizer has no effect without the Holy Spirit. Without the Holy Spirit the most convincing dialectic has no power over the heart of man. Without Him the most highly developed schemas resting on a sociological or psychological basis are quickly seen to be quite valueless. . . .

It is not by chance that the great inauguration of evangelization took place on the morning of Pentecost, under the inspiration of the Spirit. It must be said that the Holy Spirit is the principal agent of evangelization.[102]

The Holy Spirit, who empowers our evangelization, as we've seen also dispenses charismatic gifts like the gift of healing. In his 1993 encyclical *Veritatis Splendor*, Pope St. John Paul II quoted the third century theologian Novatian thus:

[It is the Holy Spirit who] confirmed the hearts and minds of the disciples, who revealed the mysteries of the Gospel, who shed upon them the light of things divine. Strengthened by his gift, they did not fear either prisons or chains for the name of the Lord; indeed they even trampled upon the powers and torments of the world, armed and strengthened by him, having in themselves the gifts which this same Spirit bestows and directs like jewels to the Church, the Bride of Christ. It is in fact he who raises up prophets in the Church, instructs teachers, guides tongues, works wonders and healings, accomplishes miracles, grants the discernment of spirits, assigns governance, inspires counsels, distributes and harmonizes every other charismatic gift. In this way he completes and perfects the Lord's Church everywhere and in all things.[103]

Saint Paul Evangelization Institute's "Acts 4 Prayer"

In view of all this, again, we must pray that the Holy Spirit will come down and fill us, endowing us with his virtues, gifts, and charisms; especially that we might receive wisdom and boldness in proclaiming the gospel, and be given the charism of healing to accompany our proclamation, in all discernment and charity. Do this in your personal prayer, in groups, and also have mature Catholics who are already exercising these gifts to pray over you.

The following prayer is based on the prayer of the apostles and disciples in Acts 4, which we discussed above. While similar in structure and repeating some of the same words and phrases, this prayer is adapted to our current circumstances. As you move forward in your efforts of evangelization, "earnestly desiring spiritual gifts," you may make use of it as you wish.

Eternal Father, who made heaven and the earth and the sea and everything in them, your Son Jesus Christ, after he had risen from the dead, told his apostles, "Go into the whole world and preach the gospel to the whole creation. And these signs will accompany those who believe: they will lay their hands on the sick, and they will recover." Truly, Lord, in our time we need such signs to confirm the proclamation of the gospel. Our world has turned its back on you, and is dying for lack of your word. And we ourselves have been lukewarm, unprofitable servants. Lord, look then upon us in our need, and fill us with the Holy Spirit. Give us holy fear, humility, wisdom, charity, and zeal. Grant us to speak your word with all boldness, and in the name of your Son Jesus, perform healing and other signs in our midst, so that the world may again believe.

In the following chapter, we will give some instructions for making healing prayer part of your evangelization efforts.

Chapter 5

POWER EVANGELIZATION

In Christ Jesus, then, I have reason to be proud of my work for God. For I will not venture to speak of anything except **what Christ has wrought through me** to win obedience from the Gentiles, by word and deed, by the **power** of signs and wonders, by the **power** of the Holy Spirit, so that from Jerusalem and as far round as Illyricum I have fully preached the gospel of Christ, . . . as it is written, "They shall see who have never been told of him, and they shall understand who have never heard of him."
> —The Letter of St. Paul to the Romans 15:17-19, 21
> (emphasis added)

When I came to you, brethren, I did not come proclaiming to you the testimony of God in lofty words or wisdom. For I decided to know nothing among you except Jesus Christ and him crucified. And I was with you in weakness and in much fear and trembling; and my speech and my message were not in plausible words of wisdom, but **in demonstration of the Spirit and of power**, that your faith might not rest in the wisdom of men but **in the power of God.**
> —The First Letter of St. Paul to the Corinthians 2:1-5
> (emphasis added)

In the first passage above, from the letter to the Romans, St. Paul makes it clear that his success in the work of evangelization was wrought by Jesus Christ within him. "By word and deed, by the **power** of signs and wonders, by the **power** of the Holy Spirit," through St. Paul, Jesus "won obedience" from people who were formerly disobedient to God.

In the second passage above, from the First Letter to the Corinthians, with which we also began our introductory chapter, St. Paul distinguishes between the way in which he preached the gospel, and another, more "human" way of doing so. "My speech and my message," he writes, "were not in plausible words of wisdom, but in demonstration of the Spirit and of **power**, that your faith might not rest in the wisdom of men but in the **power** of God."

What, then, is the way in which St. Paul, the patron of our apostolate, preached the gospel? And what is the "human" way to preach the gospel, from which he distinguished it? There are, indeed, forms of preaching the gospel, which do not lose their value for the kingdom simply by being imperfect, or being imperfectly (or even badly) motivated. Case in point, when St. Paul mentions those who preached Christ "from envy and rivalry," he does not wish them to cease and desist, but rejoices that "whether in pretense or in truth, Christ is proclaimed" (see Philippians 1:15-18).

There are surely many ways to preach the gospel. Think also about the difference between hearing the gospel preached in an academic way by a professor, in an emotional way by a fiery lay speaker, or as a carefully crafted argument by a priest trained in rhetoric. Think of the gospel being made known through deeds of charity coupled with a mere paragraph worth of words, or through a twenty-eight page treatise explaining the development of God's plan from the Old Testament to the New. Think of a friend sharing his testimony with a friend over a pitcher of craft beer, or a street evangelist sharing it with a total stranger outside the train station.

However we preach the gospel, it seems that the real choice (if we follow the passage from 1 Corinthians) is between preaching the gospel with "the wisdom of men" and preaching it "in demonstration of the Spirit and of **power**." Or, put differently (going with the passage from Romans) it is between preaching the gospel as an instrument of Christ, "by word and deed, by the **power** of signs and wonders, by the **power** of the Holy Spirit," . . . *or not.*

The difference is between evangelization, and what we might call "power evangelization," following the double use of the word "power" in each of these passages from St. Paul. This "power evangelization" is distinguished by the special help of the Holy Spirit, and the special activity of Jesus Christ working through us. *With "power evangelization," we are relying upon the power of God, and his power is being made manifest through us.* This kind of evangelization, in a real sense, is a "joint effort" between us and God: we are following, and God is leading the way. At its best, God leads everything: the speaking, the listening, the proclamation, the prayer, the follow-up—everything. We're the car, the Holy Spirit is the engine, and Christ is sitting in the driver's seat. God is working through us.

But what does this look like concretely? We can be lively instruments in the hands of God for signs and wonders, but also in many other ways. Consider those times when you receive a special inspiration that bears the marks of having come from God. One of our evangelists, for example, had this experience:

I met a guy in McDonalds a few years ago. We got to talking while we were both waiting in line. He told me that he doesn't believe in God because, as a science teacher, he "knows" that mankind always ascribed to God whatever they couldn't explain about the universe; that belief in God is just a fill-in for what we don't know—a "god-of-the-gaps." He argued that as mankind learned more about how the universe worked, they needed God less and less.

The two of us ended up having lunch together. I had all kinds of apologetic arguments to use with him—how the Christian view of the world was especially conducive to the development of empirical science, how the Catholic Church was the patron of the sciences, how the Church built the Western university system, how the classical Christian conception of God makes the "god-of-the-gaps" argument irrelevant— but instead, I found myself led by the Holy Spirit to talk to him about the charity of the Church through Mother Teresa. I had no idea why. To this he responded, "You're absolutely right. I've never thought about that before." Long story short: he ended up joining RCIA and becoming Catholic.

He had apparently built a wall around his heart, using science to keep God out, but science wasn't really the point. So the Holy Spirit just showed up, passed through the wall, and ministered directly to his heart.

Whenever the Holy Spirit just "shows up" during evangelization, you know that you have power evangelization. But of course, the Holy Spirit "showing up" takes many forms, in the one who evangelizes and the one who is evangelized. We might passively receive an inspiration from God as in the story above, but we might also find ourselves filled with a spiritual vitality and charisma that savors of God and shines through in what we say or do. We might find ourselves filled with Christlike compassion for someone, or given a joyful confidence in the Holy Spirit. The person who receives our words and deeds might receive them with immediate joy leading to repentance, with a grace-inspired open, reflective spirit that "ponders these things in the heart" (see Luke 2:19), or with disquiet of conscience leading to the opportunity to repent (see John 16:8). In all such cases, and more, we can say that in a supernatural way, the Holy Spirit "shows up" and does his work.

In previous sections, we laid scriptural, historical, and magisterial foundations for healing in evangelization, practical instructions of how to put healing prayer into practice, and a scriptural background and directions for seeking that charism in prayer. Effective healing prayer is, of course, an often wonderful form of power evangelization. With Christ's help, we can practice healing prayer in our evangelizing efforts. But we must rely upon him radically and believe that he can do amazing things through us because he is all-powerful.

And when we say "all-powerful," we mean it. Christ says that through our faith in him, we can move mountains. *Through him, we can remove pain, stop infection, and even recreate cartilage and other tissues of the human body.* Here is a testimony from one of our evangelists:

He told us he was suffering from severe leg and back pain. This pain was a result of the fact that the cartilage in his right hip had deteriorated, and he had bone on bone where the right leg met the hip. He told us that he was going to need surgery.

I asked him what his level of pain was, and he said five out of ten. So first of all we prayed once for the back pain to leave. I just offered a simple prayer: "Lord, we just ask for the pain to go. Pain, leave now, in the name of Jesus!" After that, the pain went from a five to a one. Then, as he was walking around, I noticed that he had a limp. I asked him about it, and he said that one leg was shorter than the other because of the missing cartilage in his right hip, so I had him sit down, and we just prayed that the leg would lengthen, and that the cartilage would be restored. As I was praying, his leg started to tingle and shake, and get a sensation of heat through it. I then looked at his legs, and they appeared to be the same length at the heels. He stood up and started walking around. He started moving his leg around in all sorts of different ways, and telling us that he couldn't make any of those sorts of movements before we prayed over him. Pretty soon he started running around the parking lot, even though minutes before, he had not been able to run.

At this point, he was really open to hearing the message of the gospel. He had a Protestant background, but after we talked for a bit, he told me that he was going to look into becoming Catholic, and that he was going to talk to the person at the Catholic Church to see if he could join RCIA.

A ✝ Ω

Here's a second account, in which a non-Christian woman received a healing in the name of Jesus Christ through one of our associates, a priest:

While Fr. Mathias was out to dinner with some friends at a restaurant, he noticed that the hostess seemed to be injured. As she walked around the restaurant, she used a chair as an improvised crutch, trying to take weight off of her legs. She was visibly in pain. As she showed them to their table, he asked her what happened. She described how she had seriously hurt her knees playing with her grandchildren just a few days before.

Later, while they were having lunch, she walked by the table pushing her chair. Moved with compassion, he said to her, "You look like you're in a lot of pain; can we pray for you?" She said, "Who are you?" Fr. Mathias replied, "We are Christians and we like to pray for people for healing; and sometimes they get healed." The hostess answered, "It's not going to work. I'm not Christian, I'm Jewish. Thanks anyway." As she began to walk away, Fr. Mathias replied, "You don't have to believe in Jesus for him to heal you." She turned him down again, and was about to walk away. He pressed in: "Please let us pray with you. What's the worst that can happen?" She looked around confused at the question. He repeated it: "What's the worst that can happen if we prayed for your healing?" She didn't respond. Then he said, "The worst that can happen is that you're not healed! But you would still know you met people who cared enough that they were willing to pray to God for you when they saw you suffering." At that, she was convinced she had nothing to lose; but thinking this would take time away from her work, she said, "I have to ask my boss." Fr. Mathias quickly replied, "Why? This will only take fifteen seconds."

He then asked her to place her hand on the table. He put his hand on her shoulder, and simply said, "In the name of Jesus, I thank you Father for [*her name*] and I thank you for your love for her. Please send your healing love into her knees right now." He paused for a couple seconds. Then he spoke with authority: "Knees, I command you to be healed now in Jesus' name. Pain, I command you to go in Jesus' name." He then looked at her and said, "Check it out!" Confused she asked, "What do you mean?" "Walk! Try to walk now," he clarified.

Leaving the chair behind, the woman turned around and slowly started walking. She went gingerly at first, and then a little more quickly, and then she suddenly turned around with an astonished and almost startled look on her face and ran back to the table, clearly not hindered as before, and said with great shock on her face, "Who *are* you?" Fr. Mathias answered simply, "I am a Christian, and Jesus Christ is the Son of God; he is risen from the dead, and he is the long-awaited Messiah. . . ." He briefly proclaimed the gospel to her. She just stood there in complete amazement and confusion, checking her leg out and saying, "But I don't even believe in Jesus!" Then Fr. Mathias said, "Jesus believes in you. He is real and he loves you and wants a relationship with you!"

A ✝ Ω

As we've made clear before, any baptized person—clergy or laity—can pray for healing and trust that God might show forth His power and love in this way through them; but if you have discovered a special charism for healing, or if you are discerning one, it is all the more appropriate to step out in faith, with the authority of Jesus, and pray for the blind, that they might see; for the lame, that they might walk; and for the sick, that they might be cured. There is nothing to fear: God is good, and through the instrumentality of your expectant faith, if it be God's will, people will be healed. No matter what happens, most people will be grateful for the prayer and touched by your concern.

In the following pages we will give some instructions on how to make this healing prayer part of evangelization. We will begin with some important points on spiritual preparation, followed by a discussion of the essential content of the gospel proclamation. After that, we will give seven general points about effective evangelization. Finally, we will move on to some preprepared mini-scripts and other pieces of practical advice useful for street evangelization as well as for many kinds of random, everyday circumstances.

Preparation for Power Evangelization

"Stay in the city, until you are clothed with power from on high."
—The Gospel According to Luke 24:49

How can men preach unless they are sent?
—The Letter of St. Paul to the Romans 10:15

Fruitful evangelization requires spiritual preparation. This is even truer for evangelization that makes use of healing and other charisms of the Holy Spirit. How do we let Jesus do great things in us? How do we make sure that he has "sent us"?

All baptized disciples of Jesus Christ are "sent" in some sense. *Therefore, first of all—as an important, concrete matter—we should daily renew our commitment as disciples.* Many Catholics who consider themselves as "practicing Catholics" do not, in fact, strive to be true disciples of Jesus Christ in daily relationship with him and at the disposal of his will. As evangelists, we should be leading people in making commitments or recommitments to Christian faith and discipleship; all the more, then, should we be doing it ourselves. The "daily offering" is one form of this;[104] another form is our SPSE Consecration to Jesus Christ prayer.[105]

Secondly, we should do everything we can to dispose ourselves to receive the power of God. When the first group of disciples gathered together in the temple and in the upper room to watch and pray, they were doing so in obedience to the command of the Risen Jesus, who told them to "stay in the city, **until you are clothed with power from on high**" (Luke 24:49, emphasis added). After they received power they were sent, and went out to the whole world to spread the gospel. In their watching and praying, in the city of Jerusalem (which represents the Church), the first disciples have given us a pattern of how we are to dispose ourselves to receive the power of God for the purpose of mission to the world. Their time in Jerusalem reflects, among other things, *trusting, abiding,* and *asking.*

For our part, we need to do the same. We must (1) **trust** in Jesus, (2) **abide** in him deeply, and (3) **ask** him to do great things in us and make our efforts fruitful. Let's consider each of these three spiritual activities more closely.

1. Trust in Jesus

Let not your hearts be troubled; **believe** in God, believe also in me. . . . Truly, truly, I say to you, he who **believes** in me will also do the works that I do; and greater works than these will he do, because I go to the Father. —John 14:1, 12 (emphasis added)

Believing in Jesus involves trusting in his goodness, love, and power to save. When we fully trust him, we rely not on our own power but on his. Because we are relying on him, whose divine power is infinite, we will do through him the works that he does. Trust in Jesus is something that we must obtain through prayer, and through making acts of trust, especially when it is difficult for us. Let us repeat often, "Jesus, I trust in you!"

2. Abide in Jesus

I am the vine, you are the branches. He who abides in me, and I in him, he it is that bears much fruit, for apart from me you can do nothing. . . . As the Father has loved me, so have I loved you; abide in my love. —John 15:5, 9

According to Pope St. John Paul II, if we are to evangelize well, if we are to reflect the face of Christ and make it shine before others, then we must ourselves have first contemplated Christ's face.[106] We must have our gazes habitually fixed on the face of the Lord. We must abide in him. We cannot give what we have not received.

If we are to make ourselves suitable instruments of Christ's power to heal, then we must be giving our whole selves to him.[107] Without abiding in Jesus, the work of apostolate becomes harmful to us, and less effective, or even harmful, to others. Even if he were to grant miraculous healings through us without our abiding in him, these will not necessarily produce converts, let alone converts who will persevere in the long run. Holiness and fruitfulness go together.

How do we do this? How do we abide in Jesus and gradually become holy as God is holy? We must feed upon Jesus, the Bread of Life, taking regular nourishment from the Sacred Scriptures, the Blessed Sacrament, and intimate conversation with him. Then, strengthened by this food, we must do his will: "If you keep my commandments, you will abide in my love, just as I have kept my Father's commandments and abide in his love" (John 15:10).

3. Ask Jesus

If you abide in me, and my words abide in you, **ask** whatever you will, and it shall be done for you.   —John 15:7 (*emphasis added*)

Trusting and abiding in Jesus are not enough to do great things in him. He also wants us to ask him. When we ask him to do great deeds in us, to make our evangelization fruitful, we are acting as true sons and daughters of God; exercising our wills, freely cooperating with our good Father.

*Even so, **trusting** in Jesus and **abiding** in Jesus feed into our ability to ask Jesus fruitfully.* When we *trust* in Jesus, we do not doubt that he *can* do the great things we ask him, nor do we doubt that he *will* do them if it is for the true good. But doubt can hinder our prayers:

> Ask in faith, with no doubting, for he who doubts is like a wave of the sea that is driven and tossed by the wind. For that person must not suppose that a double-minded man, unstable in all his ways, will receive anything from the Lord." (James 1:6-8)

When we *abide* in Jesus we make ourselves more worthy of receiving the great things we ask from him, for we prove that it is he whom we desire first, above his gifts. Prayer, in other words, is hindered by misdirected desires: "You ask and do not receive, because you ask wrongly, to spend it on your passions" (James 4:3).

These three spiritual activities of trusting, abiding, and asking are so important to evangelizing in the power of Christ. If we trust in Jesus, abide in Jesus, and ask Jesus to do great things in us while we do the work of evangelization, then we can be certain that he will come in power in some way to confirm the proclamation of the gospel. How could it be otherwise? He came into the world for the purpose of making his salvation extend to the ends of the earth!

There is more. If we trust Jesus, abide in him, and ask him for good things, we can also live in greater peace, knowing that we are safe in his care. Furthermore, we will begin to see things anew through his eyes. This peace and new vision should allow us, in turn, to be more responsive to those around us and to their needs. For if you set out to proclaim the gospel in the power of the Holy Spirit, you must be attentive and aware—open to the unique situations and individuals you encounter, ready to follow any special promptings the Holy Spirit may wish to give you. This should not be forgotten. Evangelization is not primarily about methods, but about facilitating an encounter with Jesus Christ. Every person, every situation, is different. And when we habitually trust Jesus, abide in Jesus, and ask Jesus, we will know him better and more personally. If we know him better, we become better prepared to introduce him to the unique person in front of us in an effective manner.

Finally, many amazing effects of trusting in Jesus, abiding in Jesus, and asking Jesus generally come only gradually. They are not directly under our power—indeed, they are workings of the power of God in us. God can use unworthy instruments for his purposes (the Spirit blows where he wills), but most often, and with most effect, he chooses to use those who have become true sons and daughters. We are sons and daughters of God by our Baptism. But trusting in Jesus, abiding in

Jesus, and asking Jesus are what gradually make us sons and daughters of God more and more deeply.[108]

Power Evangelization and the Kerygma

Evangelization will also always contain—as the foundation, center, and at the same time, summit of its dynamism—a clear proclamation that, in Jesus Christ, the Son of God made man, who died and rose from the dead, salvation is offered to all men, as a gift of God's grace and mercy.
—Pope St. Paul VI, *Evangelii Nuntiandi* (On Evangelization in the Modern World), 27

Trusting, abiding in, and asking Jesus, we become more like him; more profoundly able to rely on the Triune God in everything that we do. If it is necessary to speak of this spiritual preparation for power evangelization, we must speak also of the *kerygma*—the proclamation, preaching, or message of the gospel itself. What is the essential content of the gospel? How ought it to be proclaimed? What about our proclamation of the gospel might dispose us to rely more effectively on God's power—to become better instruments of God's power?

When we discussed the connection between healing and the gospel in chapter one, we said that the gospel, essentially, is this: in Jesus, the saving promises of God are fulfilled; the kingdom of God is near; faith in him and repentance from sin are the proper response to this message. We based this formulation on the proclamation of Jesus: "The time is fulfilled, and the kingdom of God is at hand; repent, and believe in the gospel" (Mark 1:15).

We know what the heart of the gospel is. But what does it mean? When all is said and done, the gospel is about one thing: salvation. Or perhaps it is better to say that it is about one thing and one Person: salvation and Jesus. Or again—maybe the best thing to say is that the gospel is only about a Person; for Jesus is the one who saves us, and the holy name of Jesus means "the Lord saves." Jesus Christ is "the way, the truth, and the life; no one comes to the Father, but by [him]" (John 14:6). Jesus is the divine, one-and-only Savior of the world—everything else we need to know flows from this. The New Testament Christians put great stock in confessing and preaching this with the phrase "Jesus Christ is Lord" (Philippians 2:11)![109] Many of us have heard that the early Christians, in times of persecution, would identify one another by sharing "the sign of the fish"—two intersecting arcs, making the shape of a fish; and that in Greek "fish" is *ichthys*, and an acronym for "Jesus Christ, God's Son, Savior."[110] In the words of Pope St. Paul VI above, the essential content of the gospel is this: "In Jesus Christ, the Son of God made man, who died and rose from the dead, salvation is offered to all men, as a gift of God's grace and mercy." In Jesus, salvation in the kingdom of God is near—therefore repent and believe! This is the gospel we are to proclaim. This is the kerygma.

It is important for us, therefore, to keep this idea of "salvation in Jesus Christ" at the forefront of our minds whenever we engage in evangelization. The rest of the job (often as we evangelize, but especially as initial instructions in the faith commence and in day-to-day pastoral work) will be to unpack its meaning. If we start with the above statement, "In Jesus, the saving promises of God are fulfilled; the kingdom of God is near; faith in him and repentance from sin are the proper response to this message," we will unpack its meaning by answering questions like Who is God? Who is Jesus Christ, and how did he save us? What is the kingdom of God? What did God promise us, what is the salvation he offers, and what is it salvation from? What does it mean to have faith in Jesus? Why do we need to repent? From what should we repent? In answering these questions, we move on quickly to a basic account of the divinity, incarnation, life, preaching, miracles, death, resurrection, appearances, and ascension of Jesus; to God as Father, Son, and Holy Spirit; to grace and the sinful state of fallen mankind; to elements of sacred history from the creation to Pentecost and the preaching, teaching, and martyrdom of the apostles; to death, judgment, heaven, and hell; and to many other central, related topics concerning repentance, faith, Baptism, and the Christian life of grace.[111] Normally, most of these elements of Christian faith will be taught during follow-up at the parish or elsewhere. When they serve, however, to help us communicate to the people we encounter this central message of salvation in Jesus, they will be part of evangelization itself. Among these topics, the divinity and incarnation of Jesus, and his life, preaching, miracles, suffering, death, burial, resurrection, appearances, ascension, and sending of the Holy Spirit will always have special importance in the proclamation.

We wish to make a related, second main point about the gospel, focusing in on the second part of the gospel's original formulation, the phrase "repent and believe." If the gospel first and foremost concerns salvation in Jesus Christ, it secondarily has to do with the repentance and new life of faith by which men and women, through Baptism and the gift of God's grace, must take hold of this salvation and repudiate evil in their lives. Accordingly, in *Evangelii Nuntiandi*, Pope St. Paul VI wrote that the essence of evangelization is "the proclamation of salvation in Jesus Christ and the response of a person in faith."[112] And, again, shortly after explaining that salvation in Christ is "the foundation, center, and . . . summit" of evangelization, he said,

> Evangelization . . . also includes the preaching of hope in the promises made by God . . . the preaching of God's love for us and of our love for God; the preaching of brotherly love for all men . . . the preaching of the mystery of evil and of the active search for good. The preaching likewise—and this is always urgent—of the search for God himself through prayer which is principally that of adoration and thanksgiving, but also through . . . the sacramental life culminating in the Eucharist.[113]

In our evangelization efforts, then, we should not shy away from sharing the basics of the new way of life in Christ that we have embraced through faith, repentance, and baptism—this, too, is part of the gospel!

Why should this be the case? First of all, the world needs to know not only that Jesus is Savior, but what they should do about it. Secondly, many times it is precisely in recognizing some concrete aspect of the Christian way of life that a person becomes disposed to accept Christ as true savior of the world. Perhaps, for example, a person longs to know and encounter God, and you speaking of Christian prayer and the gift of the Eucharist connects to that longing. Perhaps, on the other hand, a person is stubbornly mired in sin, and you calmly but firmly preaching about the meaning of healthy Christian fear of the Lord stirs up his inactive conscience and convicts his heart. Perhaps a person is mired in sin but longs to be free, and you explaining the Christian repudiation of sin and the sacraments of Baptism and Penance help him see the next step to take. Perhaps a person is discouraged by the evil in the world, and you sharing the commandment of love, the power of grace, and the many means of holiness in the Church help him to see that all is not hopeless. Let's put it another way: the gospel is salvation in Jesus Christ. The Christian life is the way of salvation in Jesus. Insofar as communicating Jesus as Savior of the world must reach people needing salvation in the concrete conditions of their lives, evangelization will include any element of the Christian life that can speak to those conditions.[114] In all this, the two realities of faith and repentance are central.

As is evident from the above reflections, the proclamation of the gospel can come in many forms. Provided that its essential meaning of salvation in Christ through faith and repentance is ultimately preserved, such diversity is a source of greater fruitfulness, not less. Variations usually depend upon the circumstances and the audience. In our printed materials, intended primarily for the use of our street evangelists, we have opted to articulate the gospel message in ways that are compact and easy to remember, but with a degree of completeness. For example,

God loves you. He created you out of love to be in relationship with him. He has a plan for your life (see 1 John 4:16, Jeremiah 29:11). Due to sin, we're separated from God. The consequence of sin is eternal death in hell (see Romans 3:23, 6:23). The good news is that God's Son Jesus became man, atoned for our sins by dying on the cross, and rose from the dead for our salvation (see John 3:16). We receive this gift of salvation, and the Holy Spirit, when we put our faith in Jesus, repent of our sins, are baptized, and become his disciples (see Ephesians 2:8-9; Acts 2:38). Jesus established the Catholic Church to teach in his name, empower us by his grace, and restore us to salvation if we fall (see Matthew 16:18-19, 1 John 1:9).

For the same reasons, the Scriptures also express the gospel in various ways. St. Paul proclaimed the gospel very differently to the crowd gathered in the pagan Areopagus in Athens (see Acts 17:22-31)[115] than to the Jews in the synagogue in Thessalonica a short time earlier (see Acts 17:1-4).[116] Jesus proclaimed the gospel differently to the crowds of Jews coming to him from the Galilean countryside[117] than to the Samaritan woman at Jacob's well (see John 4).[118] But the circumstances and audience are not the only factor; the personality of the preacher may also figure in: the letters of St. Paul and the letters of St. John preach the same gospel, but with very different styles. The New Testament has many longer and shorter expressions of the gospel of salvation in Jesus that come from various angles, focus on diverse aspects, and use different concepts to refer to the same realities. Each of the four Gospels, you might say, is an extended proclamation of the message of salvation in Jesus Christ through a narrative of his life. Here are some shorter biblical expressions of the gospel:

- Repent, for the kingdom of heaven is at hand. (Matthew 4:17)
- God so loved the world that he gave his only Son, that whoever believes in him should not perish but have eternal life. (John 3:16)
- I am the Way, and the Truth, and the Life; no one comes to the Father, but by me. (John 14:6)
- God has made him both Lord and Christ, this Jesus whom you crucified. . . . Repent, and be baptized every one of you in the

name of Jesus Christ for the forgiveness of your sins; and you shall receive the gift of the Holy Spirit. (Acts 2:36, 38)

- The times of ignorance God overlooked, but now he commands all men everywhere to repent, because he has fixed a day on which he will judge the world in righteousness by a man whom he has appointed, and of this he has given assurance to all men by raising him from the dead. (Acts 17:30-31)
- That Christ died for our sins in accordance with the scriptures, that he was buried, that he was raised on the third day in accordance with the scriptures, and that he appeared to Cephas, and then to the Twelve. (1 Corinthians 15:3-5)
- A man is . . . justified . . . through faith in Jesus Christ. (Galatians 2:16)
- When the time had fully come, God sent forth his Son, born of woman, born under the law, to redeem those who were under the law, so that we might receive adoption as sons. (Galatians 4:4-5)
- God, who is rich in mercy, out of the great love with which he loved us, even when we were dead through our trespasses, made us alive together with Christ (by grace you have been saved), and raised us up with him, and made us sit with him in the heavenly places in Christ Jesus, that in the coming ages he might show the immeasurable riches of his grace in kindness toward us in Christ Jesus. (Ephesians 2:4-7)
- The life was made manifest, and we saw it, and testify to it, and proclaim to you the eternal life which was with the Father . . . so that you may have fellowship with us; and our fellowship is with the Father and with his Son, Jesus Christ. (1 John 1:2-3)
- God is love. In this the love of God was made manifest among us, that God sent his only-begotten Son into the world, so that we might live through him. (1 John 4:8-9)

Catholics involved in direct evangelization do well to immerse themselves daily in the New Testament,[119] reading it carefully and prayerfully, letting it take root in them. While doing so, they can take note of the many ways that the core of the gospel and its other central elements are proclaimed there. Then they can ask themselves, "Which approaches are most appropriate to the circumstances I am dealing with? Which angles speak best to my audience? What styles speak to my heart and come natural to me? What kinds of biblical language enable me to proclaim the gospel with the most enthusiasm and joy?" The goal is to preach the gospel according to the gracious intention of the Holy Spirit, who speaks to us in the words of the Scriptures and calls both evangelists and those who will believe through their word individually by name. This does not mean that you will never use "scripted" methods of sharing the gospel; indeed, we teach them and have found them very useful. However, the word of God must truly find a place in the hearts of the evangelist and the evangelized alike.

A ✝ Ω

Another point we want to make focuses on the unique importance of the theme of salvation in the proclamation of the gospel. *Salvation is not only part of the core message of the gospel, but also the goal of the proclamation itself.* We share the good news of Jesus Christ's saving life, passion, death, and resurrection in order that those who hear it might believe, and through believing have eternal life. This, of course, has huge implications for how we evangelize. We will only reflect upon a few of them here.

We showed above how sharing elements of the Christian way of life can be useful in our evangelization efforts. The Savior, salvation, and the way of salvation are intimately connected. Elaborating on this, we can say that *among the various elements of Christian life that we might share as part of our evangelization efforts, most important are those which concern salvation most directly; showing people how to get into "the state of grace," grow in it, be restored to it when it's lost, and persevere in it until the end.* What is the special connection of repentance to faith and Baptism? What, exactly, are the sins that separate you from God? How do you receive forgiveness of these sins after Baptism? What are the means of sanctification? What are the virtues and spiritual gifts needed? How does one pray? What are various Christian states of life and vocations? How do you strengthen yourself and others against spiritual and moral dangers? It does little use in the long run to know that salvation is in Jesus Christ without also knowing in practice what that salvation looks like.[120]

Many may look at this list of questions and wonder why we're making them part of the proclamation of the gospel instead of catechesis. We get it: it is most appropriate to provide the majority of these essential details of Christian life in the follow-up stages, not during initial proclamation. As a person enquires into learning more about the Catholic faith, the usual place for follow-up is the parish. But this does not change the fact that these truths of the Christian life are concerned intimately with salvation, and salvation is the goal of evangelization. There should be no artificial separation, then, between the things you share when evangelizing, and the things you share in catechesis. The core of the proclamation is always Jesus, the kingdom, faith, and repentance; but the rest can be whatever effectively serves that core for those who hear you.

The evangelist, then, should be prepared to share elements of the Christian way of life as part of the initial proclamation when needed—though it may not always be needed or even helpful. *In one way or another, though—and this is very important—proclamation of the gospel of salvation through faith and repentance should lead relatively quickly to providing concrete information about the Christian way of life: fellowship, doctrine, grace, the sacraments, prayer, works of charity, sin and penance, gifts and charisms, faith, hope, and charity.* When these things are neglected, the Christian lacks some of the tools he needs to effectively receive the fullness of the salvation Christ offers. Sometimes parts of this teaching belongs in the proclamation and serves it, other times not. But this teaching is absolutely necessary, and the evangelist should know this.

Another implication of the fact that salvation is the goal of evangelization is that eternal life is of central importance to the proclamation. Salvation is primarily about eternal life—the divine life of which we can receive a "down payment" or "guarantee" in this earthly life (see 2 Corinthians 1:22; 5:5; Ephesians 1:13-14), but that we hope to experience with God forever after this life is completed. We were made for heaven—the eternal kingdom of God—which consists first and foremost in loving communion with God through Christ, in the Holy Spirit. "You have made us for yourself, and our heart is restless until it rests in you," St. Augustine famously wrote.[121] In heaven, we will be risen bodily, yet incorruptible, to live with the rest of the elect in the new creation where every tear will be wiped away and death will be no more (Revelation 21:1-4). We will experience joy without limit. In some way, shape, or form, everyone longs for eternal life; and so also *in our proclamation we should often speak about eternal life and the hope for it which we have through Christ; with the goal of inspiring that same hope in others.*

Some other conclusions come from the fact that salvation is a matter of God's gift, and of our free will. First of all, the gift: because of God's gift, our hope for eternal life in Christ is a powerful hope. It is not based upon what we have done but on what he has done. In the cross and resurrection of Jesus Christ, God has gone to the furthest extent to bring wayward humanity back into his loving embrace. Grace flows from the cross into the lives of all people of all times and all places, according to the will of God "who desires all men to be saved and to come to the knowledge of the truth" (1 Timothy 2:4).[122] *In proclaiming salvation, then, we ought to give priority to God's work, not ours.* We cooperate, but it is grace within us that makes this possible. "In this is love, not that we loved God but that he loved us and sent his Son to be the expiation for our sins" (1 John 4:10).

The next conclusion recalls especially our free will: while we preach salvation *for* eternal life, it is also salvation *from* eternal damnation. *Proclamation of the gospel should often include the fact that God will judge the world and each person individually according to his works; and so judgment, for anyone, may turn out good or bad (see Romans 2:6-16)—it may lead to heaven, or to hell.* We will spend a bit more space on this, because of controversial nature of this topic.

"Why must we include divine judgment and hell in the proclamation of the gospel? It will turn people away!" This is a fair question, but its answer should become clear. First, there's the argument from authority: *it's clear from the Scriptures that not only Jesus, but Sts. Peter and Paul included the judgment in their gospel proclamation.*[123] The Church and her saints have included it in the proclamation historically. These facts should not be ignored, for in every age the Tradition and the Scriptures must be our sources of sound teaching and authentic renewal.

Then there's the argument from psychology/spirituality: a lively appreciation of the doctrine of hell provides a powerful motivation to repentance and to perseverance in grace to the end. For many people (a good deal more than we may think), this motivation will be absolutely essential—without it, there will be no conversion, or their conversion will be half-hearted, or their growth in holiness stunted. To deny this is to fail to properly assess the horrible reality of evil and how powerful the allure of sin can be, and it ignores the witness of the spiritual lives of so many of the saints, for whom this holy fear was critically important.

The tradition of the Church makes the distinction between the fear that a child should have for giving his father offense (known as "filial fear") and the fear of punishment, which a mere slave could have for his master. But fear of punishment is neither always, in itself, a bad thing, nor does it necessarily imply that the relationship is one of slave to master. As with our own children, so with us: the fear of punishment can fruitfully coexist with love and filial fear. The fear of the just punishments of God, according to the doctrine of the Church and St. Thomas Aquinas, is a gift of the Holy Spirit leading to repentance.[124] Jesus says, "I will warn you whom to fear: fear him who, after he has killed, has power to cast into hell; yes, I tell you, fear him!" (Luke 12:5). St. Paul tells us, "Work out your own salvation with fear and trembling;

for God is at work in you" (Philippians 2:12-13). Although it is divine love that saves us, not fear of punishment, there is a proper role for this fear, especially in the early stages of the spiritual life: "The fear of the Lord is the beginning of wisdom" (Proverbs 9:10). Although "perfect love casts out fear" (1 John 4:18), the great majority of us are not yet perfected in love. This fear does not replace or overpower love, but saves us from sinful presumption: "We must fear God from love, not love God from fear."[125]

It all comes to this: judgment and hell are real and belong in the proclamation of the gospel. The point is not to preach "fire and brimstone": though we should speak the plain truth, we shouldn't be unbalanced in the other direction, or be unnecessarily offensive. As with other elements of the gospel, we don't have to speak of judgment or hell every time we talk to someone. We also don't have to share each element of these doctrines right away. The goal is not to artificially inject a full theology of judgment (or any other doctrine, for that matter) into every evangelizing conversation, but *to be sure that, when all is said and done, the people we evangelize are presented the whole gospel in a timely manner.* Indeed, we ought to pay special attention to this: while there were certainly eras in the history of the Church when divine judgment was over-emphasized, an objective eye will see that today, the opposite is true —*it is too often totally left out.* This is a dangerous omission for everyone involved; an omission which has gone far in producing widespread "quasi-universalism"[126] among the faithful with an attendant lukewarmness and indifference to the high demands of the gospel. It has also harmed the impulse to evangelize.[127]

A ✝ Ω

There is one more point we want to make here at length, which wraps up all of our above thoughts on the kerygma and gives them their fuller meaning. *Authentic evangelization is impelled by the Holy Spirit, and in a sense, "joins forces" with the Holy Spirit in his work of grace flowing from the cross.*[128] The motive force of this work is love, and its intention is eternal salvation: "Everything comes from love, all is ordained for the salvation of man, God does nothing without this goal in mind."[129] As evangelists—nay, as Christians—our one highest goal should be to effectively enter into the work of grace that God through Christ is already carrying out in the world. We must unite our intentions with the gracious intentions of the Holy Spirit: that the saving work of God in his Son Jesus Christ might be applied to every person, and further, that the elect among them might be "conformed to the image of [God's] Son, in order that he might be the first-born among many brethren" (Romans 8:29). If power evangelization is, as we've said, a "joint effort" between us and God, then we must know what that effort is all about—we must know what its goal is; otherwise the means we employ will not be properly ordered to it.

Let's say it all again, in different words—"from the beginning," so to speak. God sent his Incarnate Son into the world as the answer to the deepest needs of the human person, created for eternal life and love but mired in sin. In fact, every human being who has ever lived or ever will live was fashioned for the purpose of being conformed to Jesus Christ and thereby enjoying eternal loving communion with God— to participate forever in the life of the Holy Trinity. But this plan can be rejected, and those who persevere in rejection until death[130] inflict absolute catastrophe upon themselves. *The person of Jesus Christ has ultimate significance for every human being.* As the Eternal Word of God, Jesus asks a question, in some way and at some time, of every person who comes into the world: "Who do you say that I am?" (Matthew 16:15). He asks so that they may call upon him from their hearts and thereby be saved, fulfilling their highest purpose. *When we proclaim the gospel as the message of salvation, then, we become servants and instruments of the Word*, impelled by the reasoning of St. Paul: "'Every one who calls upon the name of the Lord will be saved.' But how are men to call upon him in whom they have not believed? And how are they to believe in him of whom they have never heard? And how are they to hear without a preacher?" (Romans 10:13-14). When we proclaim the gospel and do follow-up in this way, we offer people real, relevant, actionable truth—truth that opens people up to the real meaning of life; truth that drives away sin and death and the power of hell; truth that brings eternal life; truth that people were created to recognize and live in accordance with.

Many shy away from proclaiming Christ as Savior for eternal life, but prefer only to proclaim him as one who brings various kinds of fulfillment in this life. Like so many of the commercial products endlessly peddled to us, Jesus is "marketed" primarily as the key to happiness. This makes sense to us; this is what we expect and are comfortable with. And it is true, as far as it goes. But it doesn't go far enough: What about those who stand primarily to suffer for embracing faith in Christ? What about those for whom faith in Christ would mean giving up sins which have been their main sources of "happiness" in life? If we do not preach the message of eternal salvation, which necessarily includes also a warning of judgment, we do many people a grave disservice.

Why does the message of salvation from hell, for eternal life, sound foolish to so many of us? Because we do not love God enough, but instead "love the world and the things in the world" (1 John 2:15). We find the message foolish, and so are afraid that others will also find it foolish. And they will. But that shouldn't stop us; it didn't stop St. Paul. He repented of his love of the world and relied upon the power of God to convert others. *According to the wise plan of God, confident proclamation of the life, death, and resurrection of Jesus as the one source of eternal salvation has an intrinsic power, despite its apparent foolishness:* "For the foolishness of God is wiser than men, and the weakness of God is stronger than men" (1 Corinthians 1:25). Because the gospel is the pinnacle of God's saving word to the world, and has such a critical role to play in the life of every human person, it has special grace behind it. *We open ourselves up to the power of God when we confidently proclaim the full gospel in all its blunt simplicity.* And eternal salvation from hell, for heaven, isn't the only "foolish" part of the message. God has seen fit to reveal his wisdom and power fully to mankind and save him by the strangest of means: faith in a crucified and bodily risen rabbi, a carpenter by trade, born into a poor family in a conquered nation. Just as the Christian view of death, judgment, heaven, and hell seems foolish to many, so does this. So why do we "make adjustments" to the one, and not the other?

To engage in power evangelization, we need faith. Faith is characterized by reliance upon God's wisdom and power rather than on our own. *When we refuse to compromise the gospel in our evangelization and follow-up, when we refuse to "make adjustments," we rely upon God and conform our preaching to the gracious intention of the Holy Spirit, leaving the conversion of hearts to Jesus.* It is something like this notion that lies behind the passage from 1 Corinthians with which we began this chapter. St. Paul "decided to know nothing . . . except Jesus Christ and him crucified;" his "speech and . . . message were not in plausible words of wisdom, but in demonstration of the Spirit and of power," that the faith of the hearers "might not rest in the wisdom of men but in the power of God" (1 Corinthians 2:1-2, 4-5). In this way, the proclamation of the gospel of salvation in its "foolish" simplicity goes intimately together with healing prayer: both require profound reliance upon God and seek to convince not through "plausible words of wisdom" but "in demonstration of the Spirit and of power."[131] *Though we must be prudently attentive to the needs of the situation when proclaiming the gospel, as we emphasized above, our primary disposition should be one of prayerful reliance upon God's power to convert hearts through the plain, spoken truth.*[132]

The gospel is salvation in Jesus Christ. In proclaiming this salvation—its meaning, consequences, how it works, etc. —we open ourselves to the power of God at work in the world. To evangelize without focusing on salvation deprives the gospel of its power to convict and convert hearts. We'll never be truly successful in our task if we don't bring proper balance back to the proclamation of the gospel.

Seven General Points about Power Evangelization

Christ who was crucified, died and is risen . . . is the "Good News" which changes man and his history, and which all peoples have a right to hear. This proclamation is to be made within the context of the lives of the individuals and peoples who receive it. It is to be made with an attitude of love and esteem toward those who hear it, in language which is practical and adapted to the situation. In this proclamation the Spirit is at work and establishes a communion between the missionary and his hearers, a communion which is possible inasmuch as both enter into communion with God the Father through Christ.

—Pope St. John Paul II, *Redemptoris Missio*, 44

Let's go over seven points that no matter the situation, and no matter whom it is you're talking to, are almost always called for. Most of these points remind us that it is not we who evangelize, but Christ, through his Holy Spirit. *We must put in the effort, but must not rely upon our efforts; we rely, instead, on Christ's power.* Let's look at the seven points:

1. *Ask for and exercise the fruits of the Spirit: love, joy, peace, patience, kindness, goodness, faithfulness, gentleness, and self-control.*

Remember that the Holy Spirit has been preparing the way for you, and dwells within you. Rely on the Holy Spirit and yield to his fruits. The fruits of the Spirit profoundly affect how you relate to the people you encounter. How you relate to a person is more important than the information you have to give them. "They must know that you care before they will care what you know." Smile. Be genuinely interested in them as people. Seek, find, and love the image of God in them. Be more ready to listen than to speak; don't replace a story with a label. Be sparing, usually, with your words. Don't lecture them. Don't argue with them. Be attentive to their needs in the moment; it is no use talking to them about the authority of the pope or the canon of the Bible if they need someone to listen to them and show them kindness. Don't be overly eager to convert them—they are free, and it is God's work, not ours. Have empathy; as St. Paul says, "Rejoice with those who rejoice, weep with those who weep" (Romans 12:15). This proves that you are other-directed, and not self-centered. You trust in the power of God's love.

2. Be bold and proclaim Jesus.

Even though some encounters call just for the witness of charitable deeds and not for explicit proclamation of the gospel, it is important not to be afraid to speak. Be ready and willing to proclaim Jesus Christ, for "there is no true evangelization if the name, the teaching, the life, the promises, the kingdom and the mystery of Jesus of Nazareth, the Son of God are not proclaimed."[133] If you are going to make an error, it is better to err on the side of proclamation of salvation in Christ. Plus, if we proclaim Christ in truth and in obedience to our calling, we are not ultimately responsible for the response we get, but must "shake off the dust from [our] feet" (Matthew 10:14). Boldness shows confidence in the power of God to bring about conversion without an excessive need to get our words just right. It takes humility to be bold.

3. Speak straightforwardly, and in clear terms.

Most people are not scholars, and many know very little about our religion. Use analogies and examples. Do not presume that they know our religious vocabulary.[134] Be willing to share your story or testimony. Remember that not everything can be explained all at once. Recall how long it took you to get to where you are now, and put yourself in their shoes. This verifies that you trust not in your own education or cleverness, but, again, that you trust in grace and the divine love that has been poured into your heart through the Holy Spirit (see Romans 5:5).

4. Don't be afraid to invite people to commit their lives to Jesus Christ as Lord.

Pope Benedict XVI taught us to "propose to others a relationship with Jesus." Many times, we do a great job *proclaiming* Jesus to those we encounter, but we don't take the extra step of actually inviting them to entrust their lives to him, to take their first step in becoming Christians. Of course, we should make sure that they're aware that this is a momentous, life-altering commitment to make and shouldn't be made lightly, but we shouldn't be shy about making the invitation. For people who are already Christian, we can ask them to recommit themselves. This doesn't replace the need for the solemn commitments made in the sacraments of Baptism, Confirmation, or the Rite of Reception into the Full Communion of the Catholic Church.

5. Provide opportunities for follow-up.

The proclamation of the gospel must lead to initiation into the Catholic way of life: prayer, community in the Church, formation in doctrine, the sacraments, works of charity, etc. Though you may plant seeds, the seeds also need to be watered. As St. Paul said, "I planted, Apollos watered, but God gave the growth" (1 Corinthians 3:6). Invite the person to Adoration, Mass,[135] or a Bible study; give him a card with information on a local parish; invite him to your home (if appropriate); or take his contact information and promise to call him. If you cannot personally do the follow-up, introduce him to a friend on the team or at your parish who can. Introduce him to people and resources he can use to continue his journey.

6. Be attentive to the spiritual side of the work of evangelization.

"We are not contending against flesh and blood, but against the principalities, against the powers, against the world rulers of this present darkness, against the spiritual hosts of wickedness in the heavenly places" (Ephesians 6:12). Make prayer a priority. Pray against the interference of the devil. Pray for the people you encounter, as you listen to and talk to them. Unless it would be somehow harmful, offer to pray with everyone you encounter, and then do so right then and there, usually out loud. If it is not appropriate, pray for them silently. Prayer is powerful, and an act of confident, heartfelt prayer bears witness to those who hear it that God is real to you and not just an idea in your mind. Furthermore, be specific in your prayer; pray directly into the situation that the person has shared with you, in a way that shows your good will toward them, and God's love for them. In all this, you "walk the talk," confirming your belief that it is God's work, not yours.

7. Think and act from a heart of mercy.

This is similar to the first point, but worth mentioning separately. According to St. Thomas Aquinas, mercy is the greatest, most important virtue regarding one's relation towards other human beings.[136] Following St. Augustine, he defines mercy as "compassion in our heart for another's unhappiness, by which we are compelled to help if we are able."[137] Mercy includes, first of all, compassion: that emotion of sadness we feel at the misery which someone else is enduring. Secondly, mercy includes the thing that we do, if possible, to relieve the person of their need. It is easier to have compassion for others when we identify with them in some way; especially as friends or fellow Christians; but we can identify with every person we meet at least as fellow human beings created and redeemed by God. This virtue is so very central to our relationship with others and to the Christian religion in general.[138] It makes it possible for us to do our work not for our own sakes, but truly for the sakes of those we reach out to. It makes our hearts more like Christ's heart. This proves, again, our trust in God's love. "Blessed are the merciful, for they shall obtain mercy" (Matthew 5:7). Having a heart of mercy will move us, in various ways, to combine the proclamation of the gospel with merciful deeds corresponding to it: corporal and spiritual works of mercy, and, if God wills it, deeds of healing or other miraculous signs.

How to Start a Conversation Leading to Healing Prayer and the Proclamation of the Gospel

Now that we've made some important general points, let's go over some practical ways that we can start the conversation leading to healing prayer and the proclamation of the gospel. Remember the testimony above, where a man was healed of pain and cartilage was restored to his right hip? The evangelist in that case began the encounter by offering the man a miraculous medal, and he had *a prepared mini-script* that he had memorized and used countless times. Remember Fr. Mathias? Elements of his encounter with the hostess could likewise be used and reused, when appropriate.

It is great to have these prepared mini-scripts in our "back pockets" so that we can lead with them (or fall back on them) when needed. Most people suffer from one kind of ailment or another, so the person doesn't need to be in a cast or a wheelchair for you to approach them with one of these mini-scripts in mind. However, when you notice someone with crutches, a limp, or some other obvious sign of illness or injury, it could become the prompting you need to step forward. You can, of course, adapt these mini-scripts as you wish, or come up with your own. Each of the following mini-scripts involves our most common approach—giving away sacramentals. This approach was notably practiced by Sts. Maximillian Kolbe and Teresa of Calcutta.

Starting Conversations with Miraculous Medals

—Hi, would you like a gift, a miraculous medal? . . . Great! Have you ever seen one before? Here is a holy card that explains the medal.[139] In 1830 Mary, the mother of Jesus Christ, appeared to a French nun named Catherine and promised that whoever wears this medal with faith will receive great blessings from God. The medal is actually called the Medal of the Immaculate Conception, but it is popularly known as the miraculous medal because so many miracles have happened for people who wore them. Do you need a miracle in your life?

—(Person explains physical, emotional, or spiritual ailment.)

—I'm sorry to hear that. . . . You know, I'm part of a group that prays for people for healing, and sometimes Jesus heals people through us. We've had people healed of some serious conditions, like [give example]. Would you like me to pray for you right now? (Initiate Four-Step Healing Prayer.)

Starting Conversations with Rosaries

—Hi, would you like a gift, a rosary? . . . Great! Did you know that the Rosary is a prayer? Yes, it is a meditation on the life of Jesus in the Bible. Here is a pamphlet on how to pray it. Do you believe in the power of prayer? I do. I'm part of a group that prays for people, and I've seen for myself how powerful prayer can be. We've even had people healed of some serious conditions, like [give example]. Do you need a miracle in your life?

—(Person explains physical, emotional, or spiritual ailment.)

—I'm sorry to hear that. . . . Would you like me to pray for you right now? (Initiate Four-Step Healing Prayer.)

If the Person Is Hesitant to Receive a Medal or Rosary

—Are you sure you don't want one? I often like to give these to people and pray for them. I'm part of a group that prays for people for healing, and sometimes Jesus Christ heals people through us. We've had people healed of some serious conditions, like [give example]. Would you like it? Can I pray for you? Do you need a miracle in your life?

—(Person explains physical, emotional, or spiritual ailment.)

—(Initiate Four-Step Healing Prayer.)

A ✝ Ω

Remember, you can adapt these mini-scripts how you please, or create your own. When doing so, be creative, prayerful, and take into account your own gifts and holy inclinations. Below is an example of power evangelization, in which a mini-script like the ones above was used. After having begun by offering a miraculous medal, the evangelist continued talking to a young woman named Beth and her boyfriend. The evangelist explains,

> After they accepted miraculous medals, I was able to talk to them about my love for the Catholic Church. I then asked them if they would like any prayers for anything. The woman, Beth, said that she had a condition called lymphedema, and that it caused severe swelling in her legs, gave her pain, and caused other problems.
>
> I simply said, "Let's pray that God heals you. Can I put my hand on your shoulder?" We all stood together and I prayed, "Come Holy Spirit. Lord, you are so good and mighty. I ask you to heal Beth of her lymphedema. Heal her legs and any underlying condition that may be causing this disease. We thank you, Lord, and we praise you. In Jesus' name, we pray . . . OK, Beth, can you test it to see if anything happened?"
>
> Beth said she would need to take off her shoes and socks, and she did. When she saw her ankle she immediately started crying. She said that she had had constant swelling in her legs and ankles, and the swelling was now completely gone. We all praised God together, and I encouraged them as I brought them back to the table where they took more literature about the Catholic Church.

It can really be that simple! Simple conversations lead to simple prayer, and the Holy Spirit, if he wills, comes in power. Recall again that the above mini-scripts, and any others that you may come up with, serve as go-to questions and responses, but they're flexible—that is, they're helpful bases from which to build, intended to be integrated together with the conversations and prayers you engage in as they develop naturally. There is no "one way to do it," and the Holy Spirit should be your guide. Pray to him and trust in him as you put these and similar approaches into practice!

Power Evangelization in Daily Living

The above mini-scripts could be used while doing street evangelization, or in other circumstances of daily living. Some of our evangelists, for example, have used similar mini-scripts in the grocery store, at the gas station, in the barber shop, etc. They have also found it helpful to carry around a pouch of miraculous medals strung on chains, with one chain already hanging out of the pouch for quick access, and holy cards in their wallets. A key to power evangelization in day-to-day circumstances, outside of street evangelization outings, is being ready and willing to be called upon when the opportunity presents itself and the Holy Spirit prompts you. Quoting the Second Vatican Council's document on the apostolate of the laity, the *Catechism* teaches, "The true apostle is on the lookout for occasions of announcing Christ by word, either to unbelievers . . . or to the faithful."[140] It also says, "Service of and witness to the faith are necessary for salvation."[141] Can we step away from our own daily tasks and concerns for five to ten minutes to perform an act of mercy as an ambassador for Jesus Christ?

Here is an account of an evangelist doing this very thing at a playground at a public park:

We had a healing one night when I went to the park with my family. Besides us, there was just one other family at the playground. They had a daughter, who was probably about five years old, and they were all climbing around on the structure. I was a short ways off from them, pushing my two children on the swings, but as they were climbing around on the platforms, I heard the mother say that her knee was hurting. I heard her say the same thing again as she was walking down the steps coming off of the structure. At that point I knew that God was prompting me to go pray for her. So, as they were walking away, I got up the courage to go offer them a miraculous medal. I just simply walked up to them and said, "Hey, would you guys like a miraculous medal?" They looked at me quizzically and said, "What's that?" I explained to them the story of the miraculous medal, and how there are many graces and miracles for those who wear it, and then I asked the woman, "Do you believe in miracles?" She answered that she didn't know. I then asked her about her knee, and told her that I had heard her mention that it was hurting her. She just sort of chuckled and said, "Yeah, it's actually hurting a lot, but I don't know what happened." So I told her that I believe in miracles, and that I'm part of an organization that prays for people, and sometimes they get healed. I asked her if she would like me to pray for her, and she said, "Sure."

Before praying for her, I asked her if she believed in Jesus. She answered again that she didn't know, so I just said, "Well, let's pray. I think God might heal you." She looked a bit uncomfortable, so I didn't place my hand on her shoulder, but just stood where I was, about two feet away from her, and said gently, "Come Holy Spirit. Thank you, Lord. In the name of Jesus we ask that you heal her knee and that all pain leave now, in the name of Jesus."

I asked her how she felt, and she said, "Wow, I can't believe it! My knee feels a lot better. That's just so weird!" So I asked her if the pain was completely gone, and she said that it wasn't ccompletely gone, just a whole lot better. So I asked if we could pray one more time, and this time I said, "Lord, I just ask you to completely heal the knee: in the name of Jesus, we pray that the bones, the ligaments, the tendons, the nerves, and the muscles, everything in that knee and around that area, be totally healed and that pain leave right now. We pray this in the name of Jesus. Amen."

After that, her knee significantly improved again, and she was again surprised at how much better her knee felt. I gave her a holy card that explained the miraculous medal, and also one that explained the gospel, and I told her that I just wanted her to know that Jesus is real, and that he's alive, and that he loves her. They all put on their miraculous medals before they left.

This account highlights an additional, important point: notice how the evangelist paid attention to how the woman was feeling during the encounter so he knew not to be too pushy, nor to insist on laying his hands on her shoulder. Wherever we are, whatever we are doing, we need to exercise prudence. When you're at a place of business, like a grocery store, it is very important not to disrupt others or the business in any way. When someone agrees to let you pray over them in such locations, try to find a nearby spot to pray that is not getting in anybody's way and doesn't draw unnecessary attention to yourself. You probably will not need to whisper, but do not pray too loudly. Use common courtesy and common sense.

Also, in crowded, commercial, public circumstances like these, prudence may require you to skip one or more of the four steps, or shorten them significantly—especially the interview and the reinterview steps—for the sake of time or of avoiding too much attention. Prudence may also cause you to adjust your approach according to your own unique gift, be it encouragement, listening, prophecy, teaching, or some other gift.

A ✝ Ω

We've already mentioned the barber shop as a place where evangelization with healing prayer can be done. At the barber or hairdresser, you have the chance to see some of the same people every few weeks, and overhear conversations that might open up opportunities for prayer. This is exactly what happened with one of our evangelists, who ended up praying for the man sitting in the chair next to him after their haircuts were over. He didn't interrupt the man's haircut or ask him personal questions in front of the barber, but he decided that if their haircuts were complete at around the same time, then he would approach the man about healing prayer. *They were; he did; and the man was healed of back, shoulder, leg, and neck pain, caused by a condition inn his back, and sciatic nerve damage.* The man's name was Tim. The evangelist proclaimed the gospel to Tim, and Tim made a prayer of consecration to Jesus right then and there.[142]

A ✝ Ω

Your workplace and the situations and relationships flowing from your work can also bring good occasions for evangelization and healing prayer. Jeff, another one of our evangelists, was shocked to learn that his longtime coworker's granddaughter had been severely injured. The girl had suffered traumatic brain and spinal injuries falling from the monkey bars at her school's playground. The doctors said that her recovery would likely take two years of treatment and physical therapy, and that she would have to complete seventeen physical therapy milestones before returning home. After the first month, however, the girl was making no progress, and was losing hope. At this news, Jeff began fasting and praying for the little girl; during this time, he received a "sudden and certain" inspiration to give a miraculous medal and holy card to his coworker for her, even though they were Protestants. He gave them to him and explained them. Jeff wrote,

> The next day [my coworker] was scheduled to be out of the office. On the following day, Thursday, he returned to work smiling. He already had good news. He told me that he had presented the miraculous medal, chain, and holy card to her, with an explanation of the meaning of the word "miraculous." . . . She said of the miraculous medal: "It is beautiful." She put it on and stated that she would not take it off until she walked out of the hospital; and that she would give one to an infant, also a TBI patient at the hospital, who had been abandoned. . . .

On the following Tuesday morning . . . he started a video clip on his phone. We saw a video of his granddaughter rising out of her wheelchair and taking six unaided steps. We spontaneously gave praise and thanksgiving. We hooted, high-fived, and hugged. . . . [He] had tears in his eyes. He again looked at me and, again pointing at me for emphasis, declared: "It's that miraculous medal."

On the following Monday morning . . . he started a video clip on his phone. This time we saw his granddaughter walking, bending, and turning to remove brownies from an oven—brownies she had made from scratch, . . . one of the more challenging of the seventeen milestones. . . . She only needed to complete two more milestones . . . and would be released to return home. . . .

[Then his wife] was seeking to buy miraculous medals because his granddaughter had asked to distribute them not only to the abandoned infant, but to other patients at the hospital.

We sent the girl one hundred free miraculous medals to distribute, and she was soon released from the hospital, a bit over two months after the accident. Through this experience, they were made open to the Catholic Church and are currently receiving follow-up through Jeff and another evangelist, Dave.

A ✝ Ω

Yet another good place in day-to-day life to pray and share the gospel with those you encounter is the restaurant. We saw an example of this with our associate Fr. Mathias above. As a matter of fact, a specific experience of evangelizing a waitress at a restaurant was important in the original discernment of the call to start our apostolate. The waiter or waitress assigned to your table is the most obvious object of your evangelization efforts at a restaurant, but the greeter, busboy, or other staff, as well as other patrons of the restaurant should not be forgotten.

Like other places of business, of course, a restaurant requires special attention to prudence; you don't want to be disruptive. But restaurant staff are commonly open to receiving miraculous medals and prayer for healing, at least because they are in the service industry and are required to be polite, but also because many of them are struggling to make ends meet, and look to God for help.

In every case, in whatever official evangelization outings or day-to-day circumstances you find yourself, you will need to do your best, with the help of the Holy Spirit, to identify the right approach to take, and assess the needs of the situation and of the person you are talking to, while taking account of your own gifts, weaknesses, and dispositions. We can't possibly do this work of discernment for you, but we hope that these general principles, prepared scripts, real-life examples, and useful pointers will help you along. Remember, "The true apostle is on the lookout for occasions of announcing Christ by word."

A ✝ Ω

Before we wrap up the main body of this book, we would like to share one more example of power evangelization: the healing of the man confined to a wheelchair that we mentioned in the introduction. We received this testimony from Patrick, one of our team leaders, who had been exercising a charism of healing for some time previously. Sharing the story of this truly amazing healing of multiple conditions has the added benefit of showing how the charism of prophecy can work together with the charism of healing.[143]

In addition to being a street evangelist, Patrick was also the director of a parish youth group. Teens from the youth group were doing street evangelization and inviting people to attend a Nightfever event that evening, where the doors of a local church were open to all. People are given candles and the opportunity to pray, talk, sing, and worship Christ in the Blessed Sacrament. They met Willie, talked to him, gave him a rosary, and invited him to Nightfever. Patrick tells the story:[144]

I was in the church at one point, and one of the students came up and said, "Hey, Patrick, you've gotta meet Willie." They had already told me about him, and they were really excited that he had promised to come and had actually shown up. He'd used his motorized wheelchair to get himself there, and so the group of students from my youth group brought me up to Willie and said, "Patrick, this is Willie." And I said, "Hi Willie, nice to meet you." We had a little small talk, and then I said, "Alright, Willie, is there anything we can pray for you for?" And he said, "Yeah, I'm hungry, I need food, and I need money." And I just looked at him, and I said, "How would you like to walk?" Basically, those words came out of my mouth before I really comprehended what I was asking him. And he said, "What?" And I said, "Yeah! Do you think Jesus could heal you?" And he said, "I don't know. . . . I haven't been able to walk in seven years." . . . [He had been shot in the spine, and he got reconstructive surgery that repaired it, but he had pain complications from the injury. The inability to walk was related to complications from the injury.] And I said, "Well, do you want to pray?" And he said, "Sure."

So then I decided to have him close his eyes and ask the Lord, "Jesus, do you want to heal me?" And he repeated that question, "Jesus, do you want to heal me?" I waited a minute, and I said, "Willie, is anything coming to your mind or your heart?" And he said, "Nope, not getting anything." And then I got prompted to ask him, "Willie, ask Jesus this question, ask him, 'Is there anyone I need to forgive right now?'" And he asked the question "Is there anyone I need to forgive?" Then he broke down and started crying, and he said, "I have so many people I need to forgive." And for the next fifteen minutes he described how his wife had left him, and his seven kids had left him, that he's lonely, by himself, and he talked about the men [in the military that] abused him, . . . and stuff like that. I took him through prayers of forgiveness, and it was powerful; it was like he was cracking himself open for the first time. And so after he finished that, I said, "Willie, ask Jesus again, 'Jesus, do you want to heal me?'" And he asked the question, and he looked up and smiled, and he said, "He said 'yes,' he said 'yes!'" He got that confirmation in prayer. And so I said "OK," and started to go to pray for his legs, and he said, "No, pray for my arthritis; I've got arthritis in my hands." And I said, "OK."

I closed my eyes, and I asked the Lord, "How do you want to heal his arthritis?" And I started seeing an image of Willie ballroom dancing, but as a younger man, with a woman who might have been his wife at the time. . . . I doubted it because I didn't see Willie as a ballroom dancer. But I opened my eyes and I said, "Willie, when you were a younger man, did you used to like to dance, before your injury?" . . . And he looked up with a big smile, and said, "I used to love to ballroom dance with my wife. We used to go to the club, and ballroom dance and we loved it." And I just started chuckling, and then I took one of the girls by me— she was a college student—and I asked her if she could take his hands and kind of sway them back and forth like they were dancing. As she started doing that, he looked up, and said, "Oh my gosh! I can make a fist. It's like something just came out of my hand, and I feel great." And he started clapping, and then we took a praise break.

I said, "Well, what's next?" And he said, "Pray for my legs." . . . Then we prayed for his legs, and we asked the Lord how to heal and strengthen his legs. And I just got the sense to command his legs to be strengthened, so I started praying prayers of command, and he felt energy and strengthening in his legs, and I was like, "This is awesome! Willie, can you test it out? Can you get up?" And he said, "No, first you've gotta pray for my back, I'm in level ten pain in my back." And he leaned forward in his chair, lifted up his shirt, and I could see where they did the reconstructive surgery because there was a knot in his spine area where the bullet had injured his spine. And so, we just laid hands on his back, and once again prayed prayers of command. And I felt something like electricity as we were praying, and he felt stuff leaving his body, like pain; he felt physically the pain leaving his body. And then he felt strengthening . . . and the pain went from ten to barely anything, like a one.

Then I said, "Are you ready to get up now?" And he said, "I've got [prostate] cancer; can you pray for my cancer?" I had never prayed for cancer before and I said, "Yeah." And I got this sense that I needed to look into his eyes and curse and command the cancer to leave in the name of Jesus. And so I asked, "Willie, I want you to look into my eyes, I'm going to say a prayer, just pray right into your spirit." And so I looked into his eyes, and made a simple deliverance prayer, "I bind the spirit of cancer over your prostate," . . . and I said, "I release complete healing and restoration over your prostate, and all areas cleansed by the Blood of Jesus and purchased by the Body of Christ." . . . He looked at me very intensely, like there was something going on as I prayed. I didn't know what happened. So then, I took his hands, and I prayed one more time over his hands, like for God to just seal all of the healing. . . .

So, as we prayed, he once again felt even more release of pain, and he felt an increase of healing just flow into his body. And then without even being asked, he put his hand on his arm rests, and he lifted himself up, and he started hugging the people around him. . . . I pointed to the monstrance, and I said, "Willie, Jesus is in the Eucharist; Jesus healed you. You should go up there and thank him." And so he walked all the way up to the monstrance, and he knelt in front of the monstrance, and he starts thanking Jesus, praising Jesus, so at this point it becomes a spectacle; everyone's getting really touched. And then he walks back completely on his own. . . .

We got his phone number. He told us he needed food, so I promised . . . to stop at his apartment and bring him food. And so the girl that met him on the St. Paul Street Evangelization outing, she got a list of all the groceries that he needed; he wanted bread, peanut butter, lettuce, milk, things like that—very basic stuff. So we stopped at the grocery store, picked up all of his stuff. . . . And when we came to his house and texted him that we were here, he opens up the door and literally is jump-stepping and skipping all the way to our car; and he's saying "Look at me! Look at me!" And he's jumping around and saying, "I'm completely healed!" And he said, "Get this, my son showed up for the first time in about two years; he's here, and he made me lunch. I'm so thankful." He invited us into his house, and we brought all of the food to him, and we just started praising God and thanking God. . . . And we just drove back praising God. . . .

About a week or two later, he called me up, and he said that he just got back from his doctor's office, and the doctor said that his last scan, which was shortly after the healing service, said that his prostate cancer was in complete remission, and he didn't know why. And so, we're saying "Whoa, this is amazing, praise the Lord!" And then I got a call, I think it was a week later, where he said, "I met my social worker"—he's on disability, and he met his social worker for their routine visit or something, and he walked to the appointment, without his wheelchair, and his social worker was so blown away. And he told his social worker the story, and he was blown away, and then he applied for Willie to get one of these state-sponsored jobs. So Willie ended up getting a job at a copy center for people in that situation; he ended up working in this copy center without his wheelchair, and everything. And it brought him greater meaning and satisfaction.

After the healing, Willie's faith was rekindled, and began to go to the Catholic Church where he was healed. Praised be Jesus Christ!

Instruments of Christ's Power

I will not venture to speak of anything except **what Christ has wrought through me** to win obedience from the Gentiles, by word and deed, **by the power of signs and wonders, by the power of the Holy Spirit.**
—The Letter of St. Paul to the Romans 15:18-19 (emphasis added)

Praised be Jesus Christ, the Lord! May his servants love him and rejoice in him, and may his name and his glories be extended to the ends of the earth! *If this training manual does nothing else for you, we hope that it inspires you to step forward, in profound reliance on Jesus Christ, to confidently and boldly proclaim the good news of salvation in him, in word and in deed.* If we can do that, then we have opened ourselves up to becoming his instruments in the work of power evangelization.

If this training manual can do one more thing for you, we hope that it will inspire you to step forward, in reliance upon God, to exercise healing prayer as your Christian right. You may have a special charism but have never exercised it; you may receive such a charism after praying for it and trying it out; or you may not have a special charism but nevertheless find that God uses your humble prayers to accomplish extraordinary things from time to time. St. Basil the Great wrote, "For as the art is potentially in the artist, but only in operation when he is working in accordance with it, so also the Spirit is ever present with those that are worthy, but works, as need requires, in prophecies, or in healings, or in some other [way]."[145] Because of the grace which is within us, we share the talent of God, the divine artist.

If we believe that without Christ, we can accomplish nothing (see John 15:5), and that with him, we can do all things (see Philippians 4:13), then we ought not to put limits upon what Christ can do through us, except the "limit" of his will: "the measure of Christ's gift" (see Ephesians 4:7). We ought not to think so little of his grace; for as St. Paul wrote, we have died, and our lives are hidden with Christ in God (see Colossians 3:3): we have been crucified with Christ; it is no longer us who live, but Christ lives in us, and the life we now live in the flesh we live by faith in the Son of God (see Galatians 2:20). We are not the source of the life and power within us, but Christ is. When we bring Jesus to others, when we proclaim his gospel, when we invite people to become members of his Bride, the Church, we can be confident that he is with us, and that if we let him, he can and will do great things through us. Praised be Jesus Christ!

Appendix A

EXTRA TOPICS

Forgiveness and Repentance

Forgive us our debts as we also have forgiven our debtors.
—The Gospel According to Matthew 6:12

In the four-step prayer model outlined in chapter 3, we explained a brief way to lead a person through forgiveness and/or repentance. In the scriptural basis for healing discussed in chaper 1, we made it clear that the healing of the body is *not* the most important part of the full healing Christ came into the world to bring. Although physical healing from the Lord is a sign of his redeeming love, the deeper, more important healing, which the gospel is primarily aimed at accomplishing, is healing from the wounds, divisions, and bondages of sin. At times, these wounds, divisions, and bondages can themselves prevent other kinds of healing. For those carrying heavy burdens, the acts of forgiveness and repentance can lead to spiritual, emotional, and even physical healing. It is extremely important to help people make these acts, both for healing in evangelization, as well as for evangelization in general.

It is especially important in cases where a person's condition was caused by another person toward whom they might hold resentment; or in cases where the condition seems to have been caused by their own sins. Uncovering these kinds of causal connections is one of the purposes behind the initial interview and reinterview steps. For example, if you determine that a person's migraine headaches and severe neck pain came from an injury sustained in a car accident caused by a drunk driver, it would be important to ask if the person with the injury has forgiven the drunk driver. If not, you would want to lead the person in a prayer of forgiveness before praying for healing.

If a person has a condition that is often caused by self or others, or that seems mysterious, you may ask if they know the cause or if they think that any sin of theirs might have contributed to it; if something comes up, you may then lead them through prayers of repentance. For example, if the person reveals that their liver damage was from alcohol abuse, you may ask if they would like to ask God for forgiveness for abusing alcohol and causing damage to their body. If the sin is ongoing, you could also ask the person to make a firm purpose of amendment to stop abusing their body. Just lead them in a simple prayer of repentance as you move forward with the healing prayer. You could have them pray aloud if they are comfortable doing that, or silently to themselves. If appropriate, after addressing the sin that seems especially connected to the condition you could ask them if there are any other sins in their life they would like to repent of. If they say yes, you can have them silently pray a prayer of repentance for each sin that comes to mind, or for all of their sins in general.

These steps are particularly called for when you have a little more time with a person, and where it is clear that they could be open to them. In some situations, especially when a person is not Christian, God will perform a miracle to inspire repentance and conversion afterward. Be attentive to the promptings of the Holy Spirit.

We have found that healing prayer can be more fruitful when you lead a person to make acts of forgiveness to the people who have harmed them and repentance of the sin in their lives (either specific serious sin, or sin in a general way). It is not unusual to lead someone in the acts of forgiveness and repentance and for them to break out in tears as they are delivered of emotional or spiritual bondage. Sometimes a healing will occur immediately upon the person making acts of forgiveness or repentance, without the need for further healing prayer.

In a real-life example, an SPSE evangelist prayed for a woman who had been legally blind from the age of seven. He prayed for her eyes several times without success. Then he felt inspired to ask the woman if she knew what caused the condition, or if anything traumatic happened in her life around the time she lost her vision. The woman revealed that she had been raped by an uncle just a short period of time before losing her sight. The evangelist told her that it was important that she make an act of forgiveness for her uncle, and she let him lead her in this. Immediately after, the evangelist prayed one more time for her eyes to be healed, and she received most of her vision back instantly!

You may lead people to pray in these or similar ways:

- "In the name of Jesus, I forgive _____ for _____."
- "I repent of the sin of _____. I renounce and reject it. I am sorry for offending you; God, please forgive me!"

See appendix C, Specific Conditions, for some examples.

Emotional and Spiritual Healing

The Lord is near to the brokenhearted, and saves the crushed in spirit. . . . He heals the brokenhearted, and binds up their wounds.
—Psalms 34:18; 147:3

Intimately related to the above topic of forgiveness and repentance is the somewhat broader topic of emotional and spiritual healing, commonly referred to as inner healing. It is appropriate to pray for this kind of inner healing just as much as the outer, physical kind. In fact, it is usually more important, though one shouldn't try to separate the two.

What are emotional wounds? These are the wounds of the heart—the deep sadness, hurt, bitterness, anxiety, anger, fear, shame, guilt, loneliness, and other negative emotions that hinder the soul's ability to love God and neighbor freely and with the joy and peace of the Holy Spirit. They involve lies—lies which are internalized in response to painful situations, experiences, disappointments, failures, and traumas. These are, for their part, inflicted by the sins of others or of oneself, or by the overall experience of the fallen world in which we live, and often at the instigation and involvement of the evil one, "the father of lies" (John 8:44). Rejection, neglect, or abuse from parents and others who are supposed to love us the most are commonly the cause of the deepest inner wounds. These wounds can often make it difficult for a person to see God as the just, merciful, and loving Father that he is, and they can result in coping mechanisms and harmful patterns of behavior and of relating to others. Together with your evangelization and prayer for physical healing, you can and should also pray in simple ways with people for emotional and spiritual healing.

How do you know when a person might need prayer for inner healing? During the initial interview, as you learn about their condition and its possible causes, something may come up: the condition they are complaining about may itself be an emotional ailment, or you may discover that an emotional ailment is experienced alongside a physical one, perhaps even at the origins of it; indeed, sometimes a physical healing may be blocked until inner healing is first experienced.

Listen carefully to the person as you interview and reinterview them. They may not know that they need emotional healing but regardless you may be able to pick up on it. You may ask them clarifying questions to find out how their experiences have affected them.

For example, someone has come to you with some form of aggressive cancer, and in the course of explaining to you how it was diagnosed they reveal that a traumatic event happened immediately before the symptoms started. After talking briefly about it, you may decide to include that trauma in your prayers. When you are ready to pray for the physical ailment that they originally came to you with, you can just begin with the emotional/spiritual side of things.

Prayer for emotional and spiritual healing will involve (1) leading the person in acts of forgiveness and repentance (see above), and (2) simple, humble petition to the Lord for inner healing; removing fear, anxiety, anger, etc., and giving peace, trust, joy, and other virtues, gifts, and fruits of the Holy Spirit. Pray that they be filled with the Holy Spirit. When praying for emotional and spiritual healing, be specific to the condition as you would when praying for physical healing. For example, you may pray,

> Come, Holy Spirit! Heal the mind and heart of Your servant _____. In Jesus' name, deliver him/her from the lies that prevent him/her from living in the full freedom of the children of God. Free him/her from _____, _____, and _____ [fear, anger, the lie that he/she is worthless, etc.]. Holy Spirit, fill him/her with all your gifts: wisdom, understanding, counsel, courage, knowledge, piety, and fear of the Lord. Grant him/her the spiritual fruits of love, joy, peace, patience, kindness, goodness, faithfulness, gentleness, and self-control.

The above is simply an example. Pray as you are led, in ways that you think will be most helpful.

While inner healing may sometimes be necessary before a physical healing can take place, at other times a person experiencing a physical healing may also receive needed emotional healing in that moment or shortly afterward, with or without more prayer. In a real-life example, an SPSE evangelist prayed for a woman who had severe low back pain and excruciating right shoulder and arm pain of mysterious origins. The doctors could not find a clear cause, and physical therapy didn't bring any lasting relief. After receiving prayer, she said, "I felt instantly relieved and was able to move and to sleep that night without pain, praise God! I have felt a great amount of relief ever since." But she also shared how she had lost her mother three years earlier, and had been suffering much emotional pain, praying to know God's will in her life. The experience of physical healing gave her a renewed sense of God's will for her and relieved her of much emotional pain. She was previously not taking her faith seriously, and with the continued help of the evangelist, the healings she received occasioned her to get back to Church, Confession, and to start to read Catholic books.

The need for inner healing can crop up in a number of ways. Be attentive to the person and to the Holy Spirit as you interview, discern, and pray. If you have the time, and it is appropriate, you can always reinterview and change your approach.

Some important points to remember: (1) As an instrument of healing, you are an instrument of the merciful love of God. Be merciful, attentive, kind, nonjudgmental, and gentle; show compassion, and give encouragement. (2) Emotional and spiritual healing, like physical healing, is often a gradual process. There can be layers that are each in need of healing; for example, a layer of sadness and hurt beneath one of anger and bitterness. Do not be surprised if healing is only partial. Follow-up can be helpful. (3) At the same time, it is important to avoid getting out of your depth. Sometimes people need professional counseling, psychotherapy, more in-depth inner healing ministry, or deliverance ministry (see the following section). When you think you are out of your depth, feel free to refer the person and/or ask them if they have considered one of these routes.

See appendix C, Specific Conditions for some examples.

Deliverance Prayer

Lead us not into temptation, but deliver us from evil.
—The Gospel According to Matthew 6:13

We do continually beseech God by Jesus Christ to preserve us from the demons which are hostile to the worship of God, and whom we of old time served, in order that, after our conversion by Him to God, we may be blameless.
—Justin Martyr, *Dialogue with Trypho*[146]

Physical healings are signs of the kingdom. Many times, they manifest the redemption and saving love of Jesus powerfully for people who might not otherwise be able to "get the message." Near the end of the four-step prayer model outline in chapter 3, and previously in this appendix, we discussed the roles of repentance, forgiveness, and inner healing in healing prayer. Like physical healing, these are integral to the Church's work of evangelization, which is of course aimed not so much at saving people from illness, but at saving people from the wounds, divisions, and bondages of sin so that they may enjoy the freedom and peace of communion with the Triune God in eternal life. For this reason the Church (and we as evangelists) ought never focus just on physical healing, separated from the other (indeed, more important) forms of healing.

Among these deeper forms of healing is deliverance from demonic influence. Satan, the great enemy of our souls, together with the other fallen angels, works to hinder our salvation and sanctification. Our battle is not with flesh and blood, but "against the spiritual hosts of wickedness" (Ephesians 6:12). The levels of demonic influence start at common temptation and go through deception, harassment in our external lives, holding us in bondage to fear, anger, unforgiveness, and sin, spanning all the way up to the rare cases of extreme demonic bondage that we call possession. Furthermore, sin, unforgiveness, and emotional and spiritual wounds often provide the devil and his fallen angels with ways to increase their influence—for they love to hinder us by prodding and aggravating our "weak spots."

Healing from demonic oppression and bondage is often referred to as deliverance. Deliverance prayer and deliverance ministry, then, has to do with the effort to help ourselves and others become free of the oppression and bondage of demonic spirits. Through his apostles and disciples, Jesus commissioned the bishops and priests of the Church in a particular way to engage in this great battle against evil.[147] However, the Lord also gave all believers a share in the battle. When Jesus sent out his apostles, he also indicated that this authority would be given among the larger body of believers—that is, ordinary Christians—that among "those who believe" there will be some who will in Jesus' name "cast out demons" (Mark 16:17). This is abundantly confirmed in the early Church, where, as we pointed out in chapter 1, miraculous signs, including the driving out of demons, were very common. All of us, then—sinners redeemed by Christ—have to battle with the influence of demons in some shape or form. Demonic spirits are usually subject to any Christian who is strong in the grace of Christ.

How, then, should we approach prayer for deliverance from demonic influence? First and foremost, it is important to recognize that our prayer for deliverance is distinct from the official, authoritative exorcism prayers of the Church, including those connected with the RCIA and the sacrament of Baptism, and solemn exorcism, in which a specially authorized priest performs the liturgical Rite of Major Exorcism in cases of full possession. Secondly, we should be cautious and avoid getting out of our depth. We should not be engaged in deliverance prayer in ways that go beyond our expertise, authority, or spiritual preparation. We need to be aware that mental illness sometimes looks like demonic oppression or exists together along with it. Most of us are not experts on these things, so we should employ only simple means and refer people when necessary.

So what means should we employ? The primary weapons of our battle we already have ready at hand; all of us can make use of them for ourselves and encourage others to do the same for themselves. We have the Our Father, the great prayer Our Lord taught us, which includes the petition "deliver us from evil" (Matthew 6:13). We should not underestimate the power of this simple petition, prayed with faith. Indeed the simple, standard means of the spiritual life—repentance from sin, forgiveness of those who sin against us, prayer, fasting, almsgiving, works of mercy, frequent worthy reception of the sacraments of Penance and the Eucharist, reading Sacred Scripture, devotion to Our Lady and other saints, etc.—are the first and most important weapons against the demonic.[148] We should not underestimate these means. Secondarily, we have specific prayers of deliverance, such as the St. Michael prayer (as well as many more lesser-known deliverance prayers),[149] and blessed sacramentals such as holy water, blessed salt, and the medal of St. Benedict.

These means, available to the laity, vary widely. When it comes to the question of evangelists engaging in warfare against the demonic spirits in their work of evangelization, we recommend that through prayer, instruction, and encouragement, they employ these primary and secondary means of battling the evil one. Very often, it is appropriate simply to ask the Lord, in Jesus' name, to deliver the person from the spirit that is afflicting them, and to protect them in the future. One also does well to pray with people prayers of repentance and forgiveness, the St. Michael prayer or other prayers of deliverance, and then instruct, encourage, and help them in fully embracing the practice of the faith.

There is another, third kind of means as well. The simple adjuration of demons, the act of commanding demons in the name of Jesus to leave and no longer afflict the person, can at times, in a private unofficial Church context, also be a legitimate means for laity to employ, especially for oneself and one's spouse, children, parents, and siblings.[150] In regards to engaging in this kind of prayer in evangelization, we recommend caution; if one feels called to this kind of prayer in their evangelization efforts, they should seek the advice of a trusted, competent priest. One should be called to it, spiritually mature, and able to confidently speak from a place of authority in Christ's name.[151] One should recognize that although this kind of prayer can be just what is needed, other times it will not be enough: once when the apostles could not drive out a demon by command, Jesus taught that certain spirits come out only "by prayer and fasting" (Matthew 17:21; see Mark 9:29).

Something to remember: it is important not to be fearful or overly concerned about demonic influence. If we are strong in faith and charity, having put ourselves under the reign of Our Lord and Savior Jesus Christ, we need not fear the pseudo-reign of Satan. He is an imposter, and a pathetic one at that. By God's will we must do battle with him, but the weapons we have are much more powerful than his. Even when God allows his faithful servants to be harassed by the devil, as he did with St. John Vianney and St. Pio of Pietrelcina, it is so that they may triumph over him by his power. The third-century theologian Origen of Alexandria wrote,

> Christians have nothing to fear, even if demons should not be well-disposed to them; for they are protected by the Supreme God, who is well pleased with their piety, and who sets His divine angels to watch over those who are worthy of such guardianship, so that they can suffer nothing from demons. He who by his piety possesses the favour of the Most High, who has accepted the guidance of Jesus, the Angel of the great counsel, being well contented with the favour of God through Christ Jesus, may say with confidence that he has nothing to suffer from the whole host of demons.[152]

The Prophetic Vocation and Healing Evangelization

To each is given the manifestation of the Spirit for the common good. To one is given through the Spirit the utterance of wisdom, and to another the utterance of knowledge according to the same Spirit, to another faith by the same Spirit, to another gifts of healing by the one Spirit, to another the working of miracles, to another prophecy, to another the ability to distinguish between spirits, to another various kinds of tongues, to another the interpretation of tongues. All these are inspired by one and the same Spirit, who apportions to each one individually as he wills. . . .

Earnestly desire the spiritual gifts, especially that you may prophesy. . . . He who prophesies speaks to men for their upbuilding and encouragement and consolation.

—The First Letter of St. Paul to the Corinthians 12:7-11; 14:1, 3

At the end of chapter 5, we shared a long testimony from evangelization team leader Patrick about the healing of multiple conditions for a man named Willie. The healings were facilitated and supported by multiple inspirations that Patrick received and shared during the process of interviewing Willie and praying for him. This kind of thing is not strange and unknown, but reflects the beautiful order that God has arranged in the dispensation and use of the various charismatic gifts for service to the body of Christ. The beauty of God's plan is evident in the teaching of St. Thomas Aquinas on the charismatic gifts listed in 1 Corinthians 12:8-11 that is found in his *Summa Theologiae,* in the treatise on grace[153] and in a treatise on "gratuitous graces."[154] We will explain elements of his teaching here, before connecting it to Patrick's testimony and our work of healing and evangelization.

In his treatment of the charisms, "the gratuitous graces," St. Thomas says that they are "bestowed on a man beyond the capability of nature, and beyond the merit of the person . . . that he may cooperate in the justification of another."[155] Since a man cannot justify (save) another man interiorly, but can only give him external helps towards justification, he is limited to teaching or persuading him in some way. St. Thomas continues:

> Now for this three things are required: first, a man must possess the fullness of knowledge of Divine things, so as to be capable of teaching others. Secondly, he must be able to confirm or prove what he says, otherwise his words would have no weight. Thirdly, he must be capable of fittingly presenting to his hearers what he knows.

He therefore divides the charisms into three kinds: some charisms pertain to *knowledge*, some to *action*, and some to *speech*.[156] Those which pertain to *knowledge*, according to St. Thomas, most essentially involve God enlightening the mind in some way to reveal to man something which is otherwise far from his ability to know. Those which pertain to *speech* involve God giving man some kind of speech which is in some way beyond his natural powers, or some power to instruct or convince with supernatural effectiveness. Those gifts which pertain to *action* involve God working through man some kind of miraculous deed.

Normally, some individuals in the Body of Christ are given some of these gifts, and others are given others (see 1 Corinthians 12:7-

11). However, all of the gifts are intimately connected to and support one another and the whole mission of the Church (see 1 Corinthians 12:14-21). This is particularly clear when you consider the way that St. Thomas talks about the charisms pertaining to knowledge, all of which he puts under a broad category of "prophecy." In developing his broad, ordered account of the phenomenon of prophecy, St. Thomas steps back from the immediate context of 1 Corinthians and draws not only from that letter but from all of the Sacred Scriptures, Old and New Testaments. The result is a greater understanding of the meaning and purpose of all the charisms.

It starts with the idea of "prophetic revelation." A prophetic revelation occurs *whenever God enlightens a person's mind with some kind of knowledge removed from the knowledge of men, whether it is through an enlightening of the mind alone, or by means of a dream, vision, or intellectual representation of some kind—words or ideas.*[157] But this is merely the first and most important part of prophecy, not the whole of it. The second part of prophecy, reasonably enough, is *speech*, whereby the person who has received a prophetic revelation announces it in some way for the benefit of others. A third part of prophecy, occasionally present, is *the working of miracles*, including healings, whereby the truth of what is revealed in a prophecy is confirmed.[158]

Notice how the three elements of this broadly conceived "prophecy" correspond closely to the three kinds of charisms. Divinely given *knowledge* is efficaciously *announced* to others and confirmed by miraculous *deeds—knowledge, speech, and action.* In a sense, then, there is a "prophetic vocation" that includes potentially the whole list of charisms, at least those more clearly supernatural ones from 1 Corinthians 12:8-11 that St. Thomas is covering: "the utterance of wisdom," "the utterance of knowledge," "faith," "gifts of healing," "the working of miracles," "prophecy,"[159] "the ability to distinguish between spirits," "various kinds of tongues," and "the interpretation of tongues." All of these charisms are then in some sense "prophetic charisms." The prophet is someone sent by God who announces and confirms the words of God. But all of the charisms are meant to build up the body of Christ by enhancing the Church's work of communicating or persuading others regarding some kind of truth received from God. *All of the gifts find unity in the prophetic vocation.* The charismatic gifts of 1 Corinthians 12:8-11 by which we, in a supernatural way, "cooperate in the justification of others," come together so that through divine help in *knowledge, speech,* and *action,* the kingdom of God is furthered in the world and the body of Christ is built up.[160]

This brings us back to Patrick and Willie from the end of chapter 5. While praying with Willie, Patrick "got prompted" to ask him if he needed to forgive anyone. After Willie had forgiven those who had harmed him, Patrick asked the Lord in prayer how he wanted to heal Willie, and he received a prophetic image, "seeing an image of Willie ballroom dancing." This he shared with Willie, which in turn led to healing his arthritis through the symbolic action of swaying his hands as if he were dancing. After this first physical healing, Patrick "got the sense" that he should pray prayers of command for Willie's legs and then for his back, both of which were healed. Then it was time to pray that Willie be freed of cancer, and Patrick "got this sense that [he] needed to look into his eyes and curse and command the cancer to leave in the name of Jesus." During this prayer, Willie felt healing flow into his body.

Finally, after the healing had all taken place, Patrick was able to proclaim Jesus Christ to Willie in a way more direct, more powerful, and more believable than he had done up until that point: "I pointed to the monstrance, and I said, 'Willie, Jesus is in the Eucharist; Jesus healed you. You should go up there and thank him.' And so, he walked all the way up to the monstrance, and he knelt in front of the monstrance, and he starts thanking Jesus, praising Jesus."

This encounter between Patrick and Willie is a recent, excellent example of the use of other prophetic charisms in tandem with the charism of healing, in evangelization. Patrick exercised the charism not only of healing but also others, receiving, as St. Thomas would say, "prophetic revelations" from God in a prompting, a "sense," or an image in his imagination.[161] He received revelations which he tested and put into words and actions in the service of the gospel and the will of God. *A unity of knowledge, speech, and action. The prophetic vocation.*

We see this unity and this vocation exemplified in its highest form if we consider the person of our Lord Jesus Christ, who first brought the gospel and now gives us the power to do so through the grace flowing from his death and resurrection. The Second Vatican Council's Dogmatic Constitution on Divine Revelation *Dei Verbum* teaches,

> In His goodness and wisdom God chose to reveal Himself and to make known to us the hidden purpose of His will (see Eph. 1:9). . . . **This plan of revelation is realized by deeds and words having an inner unity:** the deeds wrought by God in the history of salvation manifest and confirm the teaching and realities signified by the words, while the words proclaim the deeds and clarify the mystery contained in them. **By this revelation then, the deepest truth about God and the salvation of man shines out for our sake in Christ, who is both the mediator and the fullness of all revelation.**[162]

Revelation, words, and *deeds*: *knowledge, speech,* and *action*. The Lord Jesus was in possession of the fullness of revelation, which he communicated "with authority," and confirmed and further manifested with miraculous signs (see Mark 1:22, 27), as well as with other symbolic actions.[163] Jesus exercised a prophetic office[164] in which the laity, too, have a share through him,[165] according to the measure of his gift, in extraordinary (and also ordinary) ways.

This prophetic calling is the basis for our work of evangelization, and our openness to the gifts of the Holy Spirit, including healing. As we do the work of evangelization and discern our God-given gifts and roles, we should keep this in mind. Praised be Jesus Christ!

Appendix B

FREQUENTLY ASKED QUESTIONS

Can't only holy people, like the saints, heal?

We might get this impression from our experience and what we've learned as Catholics. Many of us don't hear about miraculous healings except in the Scriptures and in connection with great saints. It would seem to us that signs and wonders, including healings, are more abundant in special times where the greatest servants of God, filled with the Holy Spirit, are doing their work: the lawgiver Moses, and the prophet Elijah (with his successor Elisha),[166] the apostles, St. Benedict, St. Francis, St. Padre Pio, Blessed Solanus Casey, etc.

But as we saw in chapter 1, it is clear that healings and other miracles were more common in the early centuries of the Church, and seem, at that time, to have been performed by ordinary Christians. And yet, someone may object, perhaps these "ordinary Christians" were all saints! Perhaps they lived during a special time!

Yes, perhaps. However, even if God's providence may provide for special persons and special times that are abundant in signs and wonders, it remains amply clear that "ordinary Christians" can and are used by God to heal. As we saw in chapter 2, the teaching authority of the Church in modern times supports the possibility. But even more, Scripture and Tradition make clear to us that healings and other miracles are by no means restricted only to those who are holy to a heroic degree. The Scriptures are remarkably consistent on this point. In the Gospel of Matthew, Christ warns that having performed mighty works in his name does not guarantee one's holiness: "On that day many will say to me, 'Lord, Lord, did we not . . . cast out demons in your name, and do many mighty works in your name?' And then I will declare to them, 'I never knew you; depart from me, you evildoers'" (Matthew 7:22-23). In the Acts of the Apostles, St. Peter denies that it was his holiness that resulted in a healing: "Men of Israel, why do you wonder at this, . . . as though by our own power or piety we had made him walk" (Acts 3:12)? Finally, in his famous ode to charity, St. Paul suggests that the faith by which miracles are performed do not guarantee the presence of the divine charity by which we are made holy: "If I have all faith, so as to remove mountains, but have not love, I am nothing" (1 Corinthians 13:2).

Following these Scriptures, the fourth-century *Apostolic Constitutions* exhorts the faithful thus:

> Let none of you exalt himself against his brother, though he be a prophet, or though he be a worker of miracles: for if it happens that there be no longer an unbeliever, all the power of signs will thenceforwards be superfluous. For to be pious is from any one's good disposition; but to work wonders is from the power of Him that works them by us: the first of which respects ourselves; but the second respects God that works them.[167]

In accordance with all this, the "Common Doctor" of the Church, St. Thomas Aquinas, taught that God may use the faith even of the wicked and heretics as instruments of his miraculous signs—not to confirm their wicked lives, nor their error, but to confirm the truth of Christ and the gospel that they do affirm.[168] *The evidence is in fact overwhelming: one doesn't need to have extraordinary holiness to be an instrument of God for healing.*

We would be remiss not to make one final point: even if one does not need to be a saint in order to be an instrument of God for healing and other miraculous signs, those who seek or are given these gifts are for that very reason all the more obliged to zealously pursue holiness. The fact that even the wicked, to whom Christ will say, "I never knew you," might perform some kinds of miraculous signs in his service, ought to make all of us who "earnestly desire the spiritual gifts" to "make love [our] aim" (1 Corinthians 14:1) and "work out [our] salvation with fear and trembling" (Philippians 2:12).

Isn't it true that we're not supposed to seek out extraordinary gifts?

Behind this question, usually, is the teaching of St. John of the Cross. St. John taught, in very strong terms, the importance of divesting ourselves of inordinate desire for all that is not God in our journey on the way to holiness. In all such things we can and often do go astray, and are subject to the subtle and at times not-so-subtle influence of the devil and of our own selfish spirit which can distract, slow down, and even divert and destroy our spiritual growth. Our progress toward union with God occurs not through fixing our desires on created things, but through being stripped of attachment to them by the way of the cross and the dark night of faith. *St. John therefore, most appropriately, puts a low level of importance on extraordinary things like raptures, visions, locutions, revelations, and prophetic knowledge, which fall short of the pure, contemplative knowledge of God.* Sometimes they come not from God, but from ourselves, or even the devil. Even when they are from God, however, we can still be deceived by them.[169] They can also become sources of vanity and pride. According to St. John, then, we should not actively desire them.[170] We should not "pause" to actively rejoice in them. St. John even discourages spending time discerning them. "One act done in charity," he says, "is more precious in God's sight than all the visions and communications possible."[172]

Raptures, visions, locutions, special prophetic knowledge, and revelations from God are one thing. These are meant primarily for the benefit of those who receive them. But what about charisms for building up the body of Christ? Though they are not his primary focus, St. John talks about these as well. *Those who have the charisms must treat them in a similar way to the above gifts, purifying from themselves all attachment and vain joy regarding them.* When this is not done, there is danger of harming faith, of vainglory, and of greatly hindering the proper discernment of the use of the charisms (proper time and manner of exercising them).[173]

St. John of the Cross says that there are two benefits to the exercise of the charisms: the temporal (the healings, prophecy, etc., themselves), and the spiritual (any knowledge and love of God inspired by them). He continues:

> When the second benefit is excluded [the charisms] are of little or no importance to human beings, since they are not in themselves a means for uniting the soul with God, as is charity. . . .
>
> People should rejoice, then, not in whether they possess and exercise these graces, but in whether they derive the second benefit from them, the spiritual: Serving God through them with true charity, for in charity lies the fruit of eternal life. . . . Love is not perfect if it is not strong and discreet in purifying joy with respect to all things, centering it only on doing God's will. Thus the will is united with God through these supernatural goods.[174]

St. John writes further that man should "concentrate the vigor of [his] joy on God," and so *"the will should rejoice only in what is for the honor and glory of God, and the greatest honor we can give him is to serve him according to evangelical perfection; anything unincluded in such service is without value to human beings."*[175]

We do well to pay close attention to this great saint and Doctor of the Church. His doctrine resembles St. Paul's in 1 Corinthians 12–14 and elsewhere, where charisms for the building up of the Church (and extraordinary gifts of any kind) are subordinate to divine charity.[176] *St. John of the Cross does not address whether or not we should seek or pray for such gifts, but St. Paul tells us to "earnestly desire" to exercise them, "especially that you may prophesy;" and the tradition has interpreted this as meaning that we may pray for them*[177]—an interpretation that seems the obvious one. Indeed, St. Paul advises those with the gift of tongues explicitly to pray for the gift of the interpretation of tongues (see 1 Corinthians 14:13).

The apostles' example in Acts 4:29-30, furthermore, seems to express to us both the lawfulness of praying for charismatic gifts, and the humility that should be embraced when doing so: "enable your servants to speak your word with all boldness, as you stretch forth [your] hand to heal, and signs and wonders are done through the name of your holy servant Jesus" (NAB). Their prayer for healings, signs, and wonders connects these gifts to the proclamation of the gospel, and emphasizes God's role as the one who truly performs miracles. May we humbly follow their example.

What does it mean to "rashly" seek extraordinary gifts of the Holy Spirit?

The Fathers of the Second Vatican Council taught that we should not seek extraordinary gifts of the Holy Spirit "rashly."[178] What does that mean? It means that we should not seek such gifts except with a spirit of humility, charity, and obedience to the will of God.

It means that we should not seek these gifts with selfish motives, nor in such a way that we give the exercise of them an importance which they do not have. They are not meant for our own aggrandizement, but for the service of others according to God's will. They should not be sought without having first built a stable moral and spiritual life. They should not be allowed to get in the way of more important things like the proper fulfillment of one's state of life, ongoing conversion, the pursuit of holiness, etc. We should not want to exercise them in ways that are contrary to divine charity or the regulations of the Church.

In order to understand correctly the proper caution that we should have regarding the reception and use of charismatic gifts in evangelization, we should consider the analogy of battle: there is always some danger when going into battle, but it would be cowardice to avoid fighting. We must not be rash, but for the sake of the salvation of souls, we also must not be overly fearful.

Are laypeople allowed to lay hands on others?

Yes, but with proper prudence. The laying on of hands, though used in a number of different contexts in the Old and New Testaments, has a special connection to the sacraments and the ordained ministry—particularly the sacraments of Confirmation and Holy Orders. Yet the simple, informal use of the gesture can be permitted as long as it avoids becoming confused with the formal, sacramental use of the gesture.

As evidence that it is permitted, we turn to the Sacred Scriptures which makes the laying on of hands for healing a sign found among believers in general—not restricted to the apostles: "These signs will accompany those who believe: . . . they will lay their hands on the sick, and they will recover" (Mark 16:18). Likewise, the layman Ananias did this very thing in the Acts of the Apostles (Acts 9:17). And depending on who we think that these "prophets and teachers" were, we may have an instance of laypeople in Antioch laying their hands on Saul and Barnabas in prayer, as preparation for the mission they were about to undertake (see Acts 13:3).

Do we always need to lay hands on people? What about laying hands on sensitive areas?

No, you do not always need to lay hands on the person you are praying for. If you are praying for healing in an area of the body that is not usually considered as private and needing to be treated with sensitivity, such as the arms, neck, shoulders, upper back, or below the knees, you may ask the person if it is OK with them if you place your hands on that area when you pray. If the area is even moderately private, such as a person's stomach, you can either pray with your hand on the shoulder, or ask them to place their own hand on the afflicted area of their body. Sometimes it can be appropriate in these situations to place your hand on the arm or the hand which they have placed over the ill or injured location.

For example, one of our evangelists was praying for a woman who had a problem with her knee. The evangelist was a man, and he rightly discerned that it would be inappropriate to place his hand on the woman's knee. He simply asked her to put her own hand over her knee and he placed two fingers on the top of her hand as he began to pray. As they prayed, the woman quickly felt heat in her knee, and her condition was significantly improved after the prayer.

All this being said, you need not touch the person you are praying for. In all of our healing prayer, we rely in faith upon the omnipotence of God, who heals or does not heal, according to his will. Though he often desires to make use of symbolic gestures, he is not restricted by them.

What is a "spirit of affliction"?

By reviewing the accounts of Jesus' healings and other occurrences in Scripture, we can gather that in some cases, evil spirits are at the origin of a bodily affliction, rather than purely biological, psychological, or physical causes. Jesus, in certain cases, drives an evil spirit from a person, resulting in the healing of their condition. St. Paul's "thorn in the flesh" comes from the harassment of a "messenger of Satan" (2 Corinthians 12:7). When demons are driven out, they are mostly referred to as "unclean spirits." On occasion, however, the spirits that are driven away are given a more specific name, corresponding to the condition the person is suffering from: a "dumb and deaf spirit," and a "spirit of infirmity" (Mark 9:25; Luke 13:11).[179] A "spirit of affliction," then, is a spirit causing an affliction of some kind. The fact that such spirits exist and at times afflict us requires us to be attentive to the spiritual battle of deliverance as we evangelize and engage in healing prayer. Sometimes that may include commanding the spirit to leave in the name and power of Jesus. (See appendix A, Deliverance Prayer.)

Adjuration: Is it OK to command the body? To command demons?

St. Thomas Aquinas addresses these questions directly in his treatment of adjuration.[180] The body, or body parts, being in themselves irrational creatures (like also the illness or injury itself, etc.), may be commanded in the sense that some rational being (God, an angel, a demon) is implicitly induced to act upon them. Specifically, through adjuration/command of irrational creatures, we appeal implicitly to God, that he may affect the change (see Matthew 21:21), or we implicitly compel demons and their influence to flee, and in that way the change is affected.

Commanding or adjuring the afflicting demons directly can also be appropriate, because of the authority given to the baptized in Christ's name. Such commands, however, must not seek help from the demons in any way, but only send them away. In no way should we make any deals or be in any kind of fellowship or conversation with demonic spirits.[181] Also, such adjuration should be made without any unworthy motive, such as "curiosity [or] vainglory."[182] In addition, it's important to mention that such adjuration is private, and hence different than the formal, public, official prayers of the Church, such as solemn exorcism or baptismal exorcisms. All other things being equal, the effectiveness of private adjuration is less than that of the public prayers of the Church.[182] (See appendix A, Deliverance Prayer.)

What if the pain moves or increases during healing prayer?

Sometimes, as we pray, the pain will move to another place in the body, change its type, or significantly increase. In these cases, it is most effective to pray prayers of command addressed to the pain, commanding it to leave. It is almost certain that the pain will be gone by the time you are done praying.

For example, a priest from the diocese of Lansing, Michigan, was praying for a woman with severe neck pain. As he prayed, the pain moved from her neck into her shoulder. He then prayed, "Pain, leave now in the name of Jesus. Go now, in Jesus' name." At this point the pain moved to her upper arm. Another prayer later and the pain moved into the forearm, and then into the hand. It then went from the hand into the fingers, and finally left the fingers and the woman was completely healed.

We're not one-hundred percent sure why this happens, but some healing evangelists believe that moving pain or increasing pain is caused by an afflicting spirit (see question on this topic above). Whatever the cause may be, experience shows that if the pain moves or increases, you can usually cast it out through prayers of command.

What do I say if the person doesn't get healed?

If a person is not healed, don't worry! Tell them that it is often the case that a person will either be healed overnight, or the condition will improve over the next few weeks. Tell the person also to trust God, and pray often; saying something like,

> You can continue praying for healing! And you know, we can be sure that if it will be the best for your soul and for the kingdom of God that you be healed, God will heal you. We can also be certain that if you stay faithful to God until the end, you **will** be healed in the future: either in this life, or in the next!

We find that most people we pray for end up very thankful that we cared enough to go out of our way to pray for them. They can see our compassion for them. The goal is that the person feels loved, and with most people, that goal will be achieved simply by praying for them with kindness and empathy, whether or not they are actually healed of a condition.

What if the illness or injury comes back?

If there is an afflicting spirit involved, and a person is healed, the devil won't necessarily just give up. If an illness or injury returns after having been healed, then it is appropriate once again to pray and to command/adjure it to leave, in the name of Jesus Christ. This can be done by the person who prayed for healing the first time, but it can be done even by the person who was healed.

Likewise, an initial healing does not necessarily mean an ongoing one. God may desire to test and grow our faith and patience by a longer, gradual process of healing.

In all such cases, it is important to be confident in God, patient, and *not to lose heart*. The Lord has great graces and blessings in store for us, which many times He brings about through an extended trial. Pray without ceasing! Healing prayer is not always a one-time event, but often it is a journey of growth in faith, hope, and charity.

How do we know when to seek healing through prayer and when to embrace or resign ourselves to redemptive suffering?

Answering this question adequately requires some extended explanation. As we saw in chapter 1,

> The same God who said, 'Deny [yourself] and take up [your] cross daily and follow me' (Luke 9:23), *also said* 'The blind receive their sight and the lame walk, lepers are cleansed and the deaf hear' (Matthew 11:5), and, 'Whatever you ask in prayer, believe that you receive it, and you will' (Mark 11:24).

In Jesus Christ, both suffering and healing are redemptive. The Vatican Congregation for the Doctrine of the Faith suggests that both are triumphs of Christ in our lives:

139

The messianic victory over sickness, as over other human sufferings, does not happen only by its elimination through miraculous healing, but also through the voluntary and innocent suffering of Christ in his passion, which gives every person the ability to unite himself to the sufferings of the Lord.[184]

Even if both healing and suffering can be redemptive, the presumption should be in favor of praying for healing. If it weren't, then Christians would normally not seek medical treatment for illness. The truth is that the desire for healing is normal, natural, and within God's plan. When we get sick or injured, we usually go to a physician, or take some sort of treatment or medicine. St. Francis de Sales, for example, teaches that we are *morally obliged* to seek out the ordinary means of medical treatment for illness.[185]

If it is completely natural and wholesome to go to the doctor, it is therefore likewise completely natural and wholesome to go seeking healing from the Divine Physician. Accordingly, St. Augustine wrote, "We need to pray that [health and life] are retained, when we have them, and that they are increased, when we do not have them."[186]

Furthermore, Scripture instructs us to turn for healing both to human physicians and to God:

"My son, when you are sick do not be negligent, but pray to the Lord, and he will heal you. . . . And give the physician his place, for the Lord created him; let him not leave you, for there is need of him. There is a time when success lies in the hands of physicians" (Sirach 38:9, 12-13).

With all this in mind, *we should not stop praying for healing while seeking medical help.*

So what, then, of suffering? In this temporal life in a fallen world, suffering is our lot. *Suffering is never good in itself, but God brings tremendous good out of our sufferings.* It is a means, not the ultimate goal. But it is a privileged means. When we suffer with Jesus, in the Spirit in which he suffered, suffering becomes a means of glory; he asks us, "Are you able to drink the cup that I drink?" This kind of suffering is the will of God for us, and necessary for our salvation and sanctification.

When, exactly, should we accept our suffering, and stop praying for healing? Let's take this a little deeper: *to accept suffering and to pray for healing are not mutually exclusive*—there is no reason why one cannot obediently and even joyfully accept suffering in union with the passion of Jesus, while still praying for healing. Furthermore, just like the acceptance of suffering, praying for healing puts us in a place of active dependence upon God, and tests our perseverance and trust in His goodness—and so, also like the acceptance of suffering, praying for healing is often good for our spiritual growth. No wonder Jesus teaches us in his parables to be persistent and patient with our requests to God, telling us that we "ought always to pray and not lose heart" (Luke 18:1).

So we ask again: Is there a time when we should stop praying for healing? Perhaps the above phrase, that we "ought . . . not lose heart," is the key to the answer. The reason that we stop praying for healing should never be because we have "lost heart." In the process of making persistent heartfelt prayers of petition, not demanding anything from God as owed or in proof of his goodness, but humbly asking him for what we want, we continually make ourselves children before him, relying totally on his goodness to provide for us. In this way, our hearts are transformed into greater conformity with him, and we are therefore better able to perceive the good that he wishes to give us in our trials. The sick person, in the process of this spiritual maturing, may come to know that God's will is that the illness continues, and, his own will having been conformed to God's, therefore no longer desires healing, but rejoices instead in the good God brings about through his suffering. Perhaps that's what happened to Paul when, after having prayed three times to be delivered of his affliction, the Lord answered him, "My grace is sufficient for you, for my power is made perfect in weakness" (2 Corinthians 12:9).

Or instead, this maturing having taken place, the healing (together with thanksgiving and joy) may finally come; and the Lord soon sends the person a new cross to bear.

How do I know if I have a special charism of healing? How should I exercise it?

You know that you have a charism for healing if the Lord uses you regularly to heal others in a way that builds up the Church in faith, hope, and charity. According to St. Basil the Great,

> As the art [is] in him who has acquired it, so is the grace of the Spirit in the recipient ever present, though not continuously in operation. For as the art is potentially in the artist, but only in operation when he is working in accordance with it, so also the Spirit is ever present with those that are worthy, but works, as need requires, in prophecies, or in healings, or in some other actual carrying into effect of His potential action.[187]

As quoted in chapter 4, the Church Father St. Hilary of Poitiers wrote,

> We who have been reborn through the sacrament of baptism . . . receive [gifts, including] abundant gifts of healing. . . . These gifts enter us like a gentle rain, and once having done so, little by little they bring forth fruit in abundance.[188]

Charisms are subject to laws of growth and need to be exercised for the fruits to be enjoyed. St. Paul exhorts the Corinthian faithful to "earnestly desire the spiritual gifts," which means to seek them by prayer. Jesus teaches us to pray "without losing heart." The Fathers of the Second Vatican Council tell us not to "rashly" seek after extraordinary gifts. Each of these tells us something important.

If you desire to exercise the special charism of healing, pray for it, while purifying your heart of any false and vain motives, making sure first that you are morally and spiritually stable. Make sure that you are not putting the exercise of this charism before more important things such as the proper fulfillment of your state of life, the pursuit of holiness, etc. If all of this is in place, then pray with perseverance, and begin to exercise prayer for healing in humble ways, especially in contexts of evangelization. You may have to pray fifty times before a gift becomes evident. Remember that regardless of whether you have a special charism of healing, it is appropriate for you simply as a Christian to pray for people for healing and expect that God might use you as an instrument of his power.

If you receive the gift, it is very important that you be continually solicitous to exercise it in conformity to the will of God, building up yourself and others in the love of God. This requires constant prayer and discernment. According to Pope St. John Paul II, "each person is required first to have a knowledge and discernment of his or her own charisms and those of others, and always use these charisms with Christian humility, with firm self-control and with the intention, above all else, to help build up the entire community which each particular charism is meant to serve."[189] As with other gifts like prophecy, you should seek the advice of mature Catholics who already practice the charism of healing for deeper insight into how to carry out proper discernment.

How do I know when a healing is not from God but from a demon? Or from natural causes?

St. Thomas Aquinas writes,

> Some miracles are not true but imaginary deeds, because they delude man by the appearance of that which is not; while others are true deeds, yet they have not the character of a true miracle, because they are done by the power of some natural cause. Both of these can be done by demons. . . . True miracles cannot be wrought save by the power of God . . . for

the confirmation of the truth declared, [or] in proof of a person's holiness, which God desires to propose as an example of virtue.[190]

As far as demonic deceptions are concerned, you have already done a great deal of the discernment if, in praying for the spiritual gift of healing, and in praying for others for healing, you have proceeded with much prayer, humility, charity, desire to serve, and obedience to the will of God. As you continue to exercise a gift received, you must continue in this spirit, letting the Holy Spirit guide you. By means of false signs, the devil will try to lead you and others in ways that move you away from truth, love, holiness, right doctrine, and communion with the Church.

Furthermore, as St. Paul teaches, "no one speaking by the Spirit of God ever says 'Jesus be cursed!' and no one can say 'Jesus is Lord' except by the Holy Spirit" (1 Corinthians 12:3). The exercise of the charism of healing and any other charism is made only in Jesus Christ, for his glory, and for the building up of his body, the Church, in truth and love. When healing signs begin to lead away from this, it is time to redirect back to Christ. When it becomes more about the healing than building up the love and worship of God, it is time to redirect. It is important to remain vigilant, and make frequent use of the normal means of growth in holiness: daily prayer and meditation, pursuing greater union with God in contemplation, frequenting the sacraments, doing works of mercy, etc.

Then there is the question of healing by natural causes. Sometimes, when we pray for healing, there is only a small reduction in pain or some other symptom, which may return again shortly afterward. It may be the case that these kinds of healing, and perhaps some others, are sometimes more based in natural processes related to hope or positive thinking than to the miraculous intervention of God.

That's OK, however. As far as healings through natural causes are concerned, it is helpful to note that God is the Creator of nature. If a healing occurs through natural processes, it may still very well be a blessing from above. And if it is caused by an evil spirit to discourage us or lead us astray in some way, our vigilance, discernment, and prayer should help us stay on the right track. It is also not strange that some of our healings will be less-than-spectacular, or able to be confused with those caused by natural processes. The charisms are subject to growth. As we quoted St. Hilary of Poitiers above, "These gifts enter us like a gentle rain, and once having done so, little by little they bring forth fruit in abundance."

Appendix C

PRAYING FOR SPECIFIC CONDITIONS

This third appendix is meant to provide additional, more specific help with healing prayer—with putting into practice step two of the four-step method found in chapter 3.

Healing prayer begins with calling upon the Holy Spirit. After doing this, you begin to pray for the healing of the condition. Pray always in the name of Jesus. You can also ask for the prayer and protection of the saints and angels in support of your prayer. *You may want to first focus prayer on the healing of any specific known causes of the condition*, which will come from any previous knowledge you may have of the condition, and what you are able to learn from the afflicted person. Pray for the various specific aspects of the condition, using the prayer of petition or of command, as you feel led. *Try to be anatomically and medically specific, if possible and appropriate.*

We will use seven common conditions as examples. An additional four will be examples of how to pray for someone when the direct complaint is anxiety and depression, when they have been the cause of their own injury or illness, or when a condition (illness, injury, or trauma) was caused by someone else.

Aside from these last four, the following instructions presume that obstacles such as unrepentance and unforgiveness, which are connected to the onset of a condition, have been already addressed. Take note that any of these conditions could be related to inner wounds and/or demonic influences, and the person in need of prayer for emotional and spiritual healing and/or deliverance to become more fully open to healing.[191]

Joint Injury or Arthritis

Joint injuries are common and vary in type—strains and sprains, bursitis, tendonitis, etc. A strain involves a torn or overstretched muscle and tendon, while a sprain involves the same kind of damage to ligaments. Bursitis involves the inflammation of the padding in the joints (the bursa). Tendonitis is an inflammation of a tendon. Rheumatoid arthritis involves the immune system attacking the lining of the membrane enclosing the joints, and osteoarthritis involves damage to cartilage.

What to Do

- Pray for the healing of any specific known causes of the injury or arthritis.
- Pray for the healing of pain.
- Pray for the healing of inflammation and swelling.
- Pray for the healing of stiffness.
- Pray for the restoration of the full range of movement.

Prayer

In the name of Jesus, I ask you, Lord, to heal Betty of her arthritis. Heal her cartilage of any damage it has sustained. Pain in the hands, be gone. Shooting pain in the joints, be gone. Inflammation and swelling, go down now, in the name of Jesus. Stiffness, release. Hands, be restored to your full range of motion, in Jesus' name.

Back Pain

There may be strained muscles or ligaments, tight muscles, bulging or ruptured disks pressing nerves, osteoarthritis, curved spine/scoliosis, fractures in vertebrae developed from osteoporosis. The pain may be dull, sharp, stabbing, coming in spasms, etc. It may be caused by bruise, fracture, strain, etc. It may be caused by some other condition like cancer. Smoking can keep the body from delivering enough nutrients to the disks in the back.

What to Do

- Pray for the healing of any specific known causes of the back pain.
- Pray for the healing of pain.
- Pray for the healing of damaged tissue.

Prayer

Pain, leave now, in the name of Jesus. Tightened muscles, relax. Bulged disk in the low back be restored to health, no longer impinging on any nerves, in the name of Jesus. Sharp pain in the low back, be gone, in the name of Jesus.

Limb Length Discrepancy (Short Arm or Leg)

A difference between the length of the arms or legs can be a birth defect or caused by illness or injury during the period of growth. Unless it is very significant, a difference in arm lengths usually does not cause problems, but with legs, anything beyond a slight difference in length usually does. Sometimes an apparent difference in leg lengths is caused by injury in the pelvis or upper legs causing misalignment.

What to Do

- Compare length of limbs.
- (For legs) Have the person take off shoes, sit up straight and aligned, and stick legs out.
- Pray for the healing of any specific known causes of the condition.
- Pray for lengthening of short limb.

Prayer

In the name of Jesus Christ, legs, be restored to healthy length and alignment.

Cancer

Cancer comes in many types. Pray to the specific kind. It involves the development of abnormal cells that usually multiply uncontrollably, destroy normal tissues, and spread throughout the body. It can cause varying kinds of symptoms depending on the type.

What to Do

- Pray for the healing of any specific known causes of the cancer.
- Pray for the immune system to be strengthened against cancer cells.
- Pray for the halting of the growth and spreading of cancer cells.
- Pray for cancer cells to die and be replaced with healthy cells.
- Pray for the healing of damaged tissues.

Prayer

In the name of Jesus, lung tumors, shrink. All cancer cells, be destroyed. May all damage to noncancerous cells be healed, and the spreading of cancerous cells, cease. Immune system, be strengthened. In the name of Jesus, we command this body to return to health.

Lung Conditions (Bronchitis, Pneumonia, etc.)

Bronchitis is inflammation of the lining of the bronchial tubes leading to the lungs. It is often caused by a viral infection for acute cases, or smoking for chronic cases. Other irritants in the air can contribute as well.

Pneumonia is an infection causing inflammation of the air sacs of the lungs. It can be caused by bacteria, viruses, fungi, etc.

What to Do

- Pray for the healing of any specific known causes of the lung condition.
- Pray for strengthening of the immune system.
- Pray for damaged bronchial tube to be healed (bronchitis).
- Pray for any infection to be removed.
- Pray for inflammation to go down and irritation to cease.
- Pray for cough and pain or discomfort to leave, and (if applicable) also fever, chills, or other symptoms.

Prayer 1

In the name of Jesus, I command any viral infection in the bronchial tube to be healed. Viruses, be destroyed. May any damage to the bronchial tube lining be healed, in the name of Jesus. Inflammation, go down. Cough, go away. Pain and discomfort, I command you to leave, in Jesus' name.

Prayer 2

Lord Jesus, we pray that you completely heal Jim of pneumonia, in the name of Jesus. Strengthen his immune system against his viral infection and any other infection. Kill the virus, and make all inflammation go down. Remove all pus and phlegm, and heal his lungs completely. Open all airways so that his lungs function at perfect health. In the name of Jesus, we pray.

Blindness

Partial or complete blindness can be caused by many different underlying conditions and other causes, such as physical injury, or glaucoma.

What to Do

- Pray for the healing of any specific known causes of the blindness.
- Pray for the restoration of the eyes, that they may open, and see.
- Pray for healing of retina, cones, rods, nerves.
- Pray for healing of the optic nerve.
- Pray for healing of any inflammation (macular degeneration) or pressure (glaucoma).

Prayer

In the name of Jesus, I command these eyes to open. Be restored to perfect health. Be healed, retinas, cones, rods, nerves; optic nerve, be healed. In the name of Jesus, eyes, be restored to the perfect vision they were intended to enjoy.

Infertility

Infertility has many possible causes, but it can be common for the cause to be unknown. The causes may be rooted in health issues in the male, the female, or both. Disorders of the reproductive organs, toxins of various kinds, damage due to certain illnesses, and general health can affect fertility.

What to Do

- Pray for the healing of any specific known causes of the infertility.
- Pray for the healing of the sexual, reproductive organs and processes.
- Pray for the healing of any disease that may be causing infertility.
- Pray for the removal of any toxins in the system that may be causing infertility.
- Pray for the conception, implantation, bearing, and birth of a healthy child.

Prayer

Lord Jesus, I ask you to heal your servant Suzy. Remove the polyps in her uterus and heal the uterine walls. Restore to full health her entire reproductive system, and that of her husband, Tony. Remove any environmental toxins, and heal their bodies of any damage they may have caused by alcohol and tobacco use. By your power, grant them the child they have so long desired, that they can give you glory by raising them according to your commandments. In Jesus' name , we pray.

Anxiety, Depression

Anxiety and depression can have a variety of causes and aggravators: biological, psychological, situational, relational, spiritual, etc. These can be passing moods or states of mind, often coming from recent experiences, on the one hand; or deeper, perhaps chronic conditions, coming from inner wounds and traumas, on the other hand. Sometimes demonic spirits are involved, usually aggravating inner wounds. Since we are neither therapists, nor engaging in in-depth inner healing prayer or in-depth "deliverance ministry," it is only appropriate to interview, pray, and advise in simple ways, and to refer the person to qualified priests, counselors, therapists, Church-supported deliverance ministries, etc., if needed.

What to Do

- Pray for the healing of any specific known causes of the anxiety or depression.
- Ask the person whether they might have any serious sin to repent of, and if there is anyone they have not forgiven.
- Ask for the help of the Holy Spirit.
- Lead them through act of self-forgiveness and/or repentance, as needed. Encourage them to bring it to the sacrament of Penance, if they are Catholic and there is a sin of grave matter involved.

- Lead them through an act of forgiveness, as needed.
- Pray for healing of the anxiety or depression.
- Pray for deliverance from any demonic influence (using St. Michael Prayer, "Deliver us from evil," etc.)
- Pray for a filling of the Holy Spirit.
- Encourage them and give them pointers on how to trustingly turn to God with all their cares and worries, and to find hope and healing in his truth and love.
- If it seems more than regular, situational stress, and it is appropriate, you may ask them if they have considered talking to a trained counselor or therapist, or a Church-supported deliverance ministry.
- Reinterview, and pray again if you think it might be helpful.

Prayer

Lord Jesus, come to your servant Sarah and have mercy on her. Fill her with your peace and strength. When she is anxious, give her trust in your love and providence. When she is depressed, give her hope. Help her to love you above all, and love her neighbor as herself for your sake. Help her to acknowledge any hurts she may have, and to forgive anyone who has caused those hurts. Deliver her from the wiles of the evil one, and fill her with the Holy Spirit.

Injury or Illness Caused by Self

During the interview or reinterview steps, you may discover that an injury or illness, in all probability, may have been self-caused (car accident due to reckless driving, sexually transmitted disease due to fornication/promiscuity, cancer due to smoking or excessive sunbathing, etc.). In such cases, you will want to inquire, nonjudgmentally and without digging, as to whether it may indeed be self-caused; and if so, whether the person needs to forgive themselves and/or repent and change their ways. It is not necessary that you know exactly what they did to lead them in prayer of repentance. It is not necessary that they make the act of repentance out loud. Be compassionate and supportive.

What to Do

- Ask whether it may be possible that the condition may have been caused by something they have done.
- If they say yes, ask whether the person needs to forgive themselves for causing the condition, and repent of any sin.
- Ask for the help of the Holy Spirit.
- Lead them through act of self-forgiveness and/or repentance, as needed. Encourage them to bring it to the sacrament of Penance, if they are Catholic and there is a sin of grave matter involved.
- Begin prayer for healing.

Prayer 1

You: "So you were diagnosed with lung cancer. Could this be related to anything you've done in the past?"

Other: "Yes, I've been a smoker since I was in my early twenties."

You: "Do you think it's possible that you need to forgive yourself for smoking all these years?"

Other: "I've never thought of that—but perhaps I do. Ever since I found out about the cancer, I've been so depressed and down on myself."

You: "Have you asked forgiveness of God? Have you repented?"

Other: "No. Not yet."

You: "Sometimes healing can be blocked by a lack of forgiveness or repentance. How about if we go through prayers of forgiveness of self, and repentance? . . . Ok. Repeat after me: 'In the name of Jesus I forgive myself for harming my health through unhealthy smoking habits.' . . . And now repentance: 'I repent of the sin harming my own health through tobacco abuse. I renounce and reject it. I am sorry for offending you; God, please forgive me!' . . . Good!"

(Pray for healing like normal.)

Prayer 2 (Longer)

You: "So you said that you were being 'stupid' before you got in the car accident where you injured your arms. Do you mean to imply that you caused the injury?"

Other: "Yes. I was driving recklessly, just for the fun of it. I didn't think I could lose control or hurt myself. I thought I was invincible. So I blame myself. If I hadn't been so stupid, I would never have gotten in the car accident, and I wouldn't have this constant pain in my arms, and unable to move them right."

You: "Have you repented of driving recklessly? Did you ask God's forgiveness?"

Other: "No—I guess I never have. I've just been so angry about it."

You: "It's important that we acknowledge and repent of our sins because they offend God, and they hurt ourselves and other people."

Other: "Yes, I know."

You: "Plus, sometimes a lack of repentance can prevent healing. . . . But you also said that you were angry. Who are you angry at?"

Other: "I don't know. I guess I'm angry at myself."

You: "If that's the case, you may need also to forgive yourself. How does that sound?"

Other: "That sounds good. I think I do need to forgive myself."

You: "Good. Shall we go through an act of forgiveness of self, and then an act of repentance?"

Other: "Yes."

You: "Alright. You can begin by saying, 'In the name of Jesus, I forgive myself for driving recklessly,' and continue how you think right."

Other: "OK. In the name of Jesus I forgive myself for driving recklessly and causing myself injury. I forgive myself for being stupid. I forgive myself for ruining my car. I forgive myself for damaging somebody else's car. . . . Even though it's very hard, I can accept the consequences and move on. It's going to be OK."

You: "Great! How does that feel?"

Other: "It feels good."

You: "Now let's make an act of repentance. Repeat after me: 'I repent of the sin of driving recklessly. I renounce and reject it. I am sorry for offending you; God, please forgive me!'"

Other: "I repent of the sin of driving recklessly. I renounce and reject it. I am sorry for offending you; God, please forgive me! . . . Lord, I'm sorry for what I did. I realize I was being stupid and selfish. I promise never to do such things again."

You: "You sound very sincere. Praise Jesus! You will want to bring it to confession as well, if you did it knowingly. Alright? . . . OK. Are you ready to begin praying for healing?"

Other: "Yes, I am."

(Pray for healing like normal.)

Injury or Illness Caused by Someone Else

During the interview or reinterview steps, you may discover that an injury or illness may have been caused by some other person (injury due to a drunk driver, illness due to bad habits caused by the scandalous influence of another, an illness beginning mysteriously after a traumatic experience caused by someone else, etc.). In such cases, you will want to gently inquire whether the person needs to forgive the other person involved. If it seems that they could have some fault in the matter, you may ask them whether that could be the case, but don't press it. If so, you may also want to lead them in prayer of repentance.

What to Do

- If the answer is not already obvious, ask the person if they think that the injury or illness was caused by another person.

- Ask the person whether or not they think that they have forgiven the person who caused the injury or illness.
- If they have not forgiven the person, ask for the help of the Holy Spirit, and lead them through an act of forgiveness.
- Begin prayer for healing.

Prayer

Other: "Yes—I think it was about a week or two after my wife left me that I started to get these migraines. Since then, I have never gone longer than a few days without them."

You: "Sometimes, a mysterious condition like yours is caused or made possible by difficult experiences we've gone through. Who do you think is at fault for what happened?"

Other: "Her! Who else would be! I didn't leave her—she's left me!"

You: "Have you forgiven her?"

Other: "I know that I'm supposed to—but it's easier said than done. She's ruined my life! . . . Plus, she's not even sorry! How can I forgive someone who's not sorry?"

You: "You know that the Lord requires us to forgive those who have harmed us as a condition of being forgiven of our sins. Also, you may not know that sometimes unforgiveness can be a blockage to healing."

Other: "It can? . . . But it's no good. I don't know if I even can forgive her."

You: "Forgiveness is a choice we make, and doesn't necessarily mean having warm feelings for the person. It means that you no longer hold the offense against them, and that you wish them good, not evil. Even if they're not sorry, you can at least let go of the desire for revenge. That is a choice you make. Does that make sense? . . . Good. Can I lead you through prayers of forgiveness?"

Other: "Yes, let's do it."

You: "You can say, 'In the name of Jesus, I forgive my wife for'— and then say what she did. . . . Good! Now, one more thing: not only unforgiveness, but also unrepentance, can hinder healing. Do you think that there is anything you need to repent of?"

Other: "Well, actually, yes. I guess I want to repent for the ways that I failed as a husband."

You: "OK! We can do that! You don't need to say them aloud if you don't want—but you can say them in your mind: 'I repent of the sin of'—whatever it is. 'I renounce and reject it. I am sorry for offending you; God, please forgive me!' Sound good?"

Other: "Yes." [repents quietly]

You: "Alright—let's pray for healing now."

(Pray for healing like normal.)

Emotional or Psychological Trauma Caused by Someone Else

This is a variation on the previous type—an injury or illness caused by someone else. The person may have come to you for healing prayer for these kinds of inner wounds, or they may have come to you for healing of some physical malady, but either way, the interview or reinterview step uncovers that a trauma was experienced. A trauma can be at the source of a physical issue, or can simply be preventing physical healing.

For both reasons, we may pray for people suffering from emotional and psychological trauma. However, it is important to understand that we are not licensed counselors or therapists, and ought to avoid getting out of our depth by trying to help in ways in which we are not trained to help. What we can do, in simple and humble ways, is pray with someone for the healing of the wounds of the heart and deliverance from any influence of the evil one, lead them in prayer, acts of forgiveness, and if needed, prayers of repentance. We can also encourage them and speak the truth to them. Sometimes that will need to include the truth that God did not cause the evil done to them, but was with them, loving them, the whole time. Trauma may also occur where no one is immediately to blame, in which case prayers of forgiveness of others may not be needed.

What to Do

- If they came to you originally for healing of a physical illness, tell them that sometimes previous emotional wounds can be a block to physical healing.
- If the trauma occurred shortly before the physical condition began, tell them also that emotional trauma can on occasion be at the source of physical illness.
- Tell them that unforgiveness can sometimes prevent healing.
- Speak the truth to them: assure them of God's goodness, his hatred of evil, and his desire to overcome it in us through the acts of repentance, forgiveness, and living life in Jesus Christ.
- Pray for the help of the Holy Spirit.
- Lead them through the act of forgiveness.
- If you sense the need, ask if they have any serious sins to repent of, and if so, lead them through act of repentance.
- Pray for healing of the trauma.
- Pray for the healing of the wounds of the heart, the dominant harmful emotions, and removal of lies.
- Pray for deliverance from any demonic influence (using the St. Michael prayer, "Deliver us from evil," etc.)
- Pray that person be filled with the Holy Spirit and receive the gifts and fruits of the Holy Spirit.
- After reinterviewing, you may decide to begin prayer for physical healing, or briefly revisit one or more aspects of the prayers just completed.

Prayer

[Prayer for healing has not worked. In the reinterview step, you uncover that the person had been mocked and beaten up by a classmate years earlier, though he never realized that he still held deep resentment for the classmate, and that the event had profoundly affected him.]

You: "I'm so sorry that that happened to you. We should pray about this before praying again about your illness. It is possible that an event like this could be part of the cause of an illness, if the illness began within a few weeks or so after the event. It's also possible that the experience you had, because it's not properly addressed, may be just preventing healing."

Other: "Well, my illness began over a year after it happened. But maybe it is preventing healing, because the doctors are just baffled. They can't seem to effectively treat it."

You: "Well, it sounds like that could be what is going on. But whether it is or not, it doesn't hurt to pray about it. . . . A big part of traumas like this can be lack of forgiveness of the person who harmed you, and also having a hard time trusting God. It's important to understand that God is not the cause of this evil. It was the sin of the person who hurt you, and in one way or another, the influence of the devil. Like the innocent suffering of Jesus, God allowed it, but he did not cause it, and was with you the whole time, loving you. Also, forgiveness is a choice we make, and doesn't necessarily mean having warm feelings for the person. It means that you no longer hold the offense against them, that you renounce the desire for revenge, that you wish them good, not evil. Does this make sense?"

You: "Yeah—I guess it does; at least in my mind. It doesn't feel like it, though."

You: "Well, we can ask the Lord to grant that this knowledge moves from your mind to your heart. How about if we start by going through prayers of forgiveness? . . . OK. Let's call on the Holy Spirit first. Come Holy Spirit, be with us, strengthen us, and give us wisdom as we pray.

Heal Jake's heart of anger and the desire for revenge. . . . OK, now speaking from your heart, repeat after me: 'In the name of Jesus, I forgive _____ for mocking and hurting me,' or however you want to put it. . . . Good!"

Other: "Wow, I didn't think I could do that. . . . OK, what's next?"

You: "Let's pray for the healing of the trauma you endured.

Other: "OK."

You: "Come Holy Spirit. . . . Heavenly Father, we ask you to heal the wounded heart of your son Jake by the blood of your Divine Son Jesus Christ. Pour your merciful, healing love into his heart. Help him to let go of anger, hurt, fear, and self-hatred. Give to him the firm, deep, and abiding conviction that in Jesus, he is your beloved son, and let not the lies of the evil one have any place within him. . . . Now let's pray together the prayer of Jesus: Our Father, who art in heaven, hallowed be thy name. Thy Kingdom come; thy will be done, on earth as it is in heaven. . . . St. Michael the Archangel, defend us in battle. Be our safeguard against the wickedness and snares of the devil . . ."

You: "Come Holy Spirit; fill Jake as in a temple. Give him a deeper share in your gifts: wisdom, understanding, counsel, fortitude, knowledge, piety, and fear of the Lord."

[Reinterview and pray for healing like normal.]

Notes

1   Thomas Aquinas, *Commentary on the Letters of Saint Paul to the Corinthians* (Lander, WY: Aquinas Institute for the Study of Sacred Doctrine, 2012), 29-31. Cornelius à Lapide, *Saint Paul's First and Second Epistles to the Corinthians*, The Great Commentary of Cornelius à Lapide (Fitzwilliam, NH: Loreto Publications, 2016), 32-34. See also George T. Montague, First Corinthians, Catholic Commentary on Sacred Scripture (Grand Rapids, MI: Baker Academic, 2011), 56-59.

2   See à Lapide, *Epistles to the Corinthians*, 16, 20–21.

3   On this passage, à Lapide comments: "The spiritual energy ... in which God reigns ... [is] not to be found in eloquence, but in the powerful working of the Holy Spirit, specifically in effective preaching, in the power of miracles, in the expulsion of demons, and ... in the sufferings of the Apostle's life ... , and in conversion of character and in holy living." à Lapide, *Epistles to the Corinthians*, 89.

4   "In the early Church ... almost all Christians wrought miracles, at least of certain kinds. ... This is plain from Justin's *Dialogue Against Trypho*, Tertullian (Apolog.), Lactantius, and others." à Lapide, *The Holy Gospel According to Saint Mark*, The Great Commentary of Cornelius à Lapide (Fitzwilliam, NH: Loreto Publications, 2008), 110.

5   Bert Ghezzi, *Mystics and Miracles: True Stories of Lives Touched by God* (Chicago: Loyola Press, 2002), 173.

6   See *Catechism of the Catholic Church*, 309–313, 324. "Faith gives us the certainty that God would not permit an evil if he did not cause a good to come from that very evil, by ways that we shall fully know only in eternal life" (324).

7   Sickness and death afflict us because of sin and the devil in a general way, as results of our fallen nature: "Although your bodies are dead because of sin, your spirits are alive because of righteousness" (Romans 8:10). In addition, sometimes the devil causes sickness in a more direct way, afflicting a person by a "spirit of infirmity" as in the case of the crippled woman in the Gospel of Luke whom Jesus heals, saying, "Ought not this woman ... whom Satan bound for eighteen years, be loosed from this bond?" (Luke 13:11, 16).

8   Likewise, this is the way that St. Peter explains the ministry of Jesus when preaching in Caesarea: "[Jesus] went about doing good and healing all that were oppressed by the devil, for God was with him" (Acts 10:38).

9   "Physical healings and exorcisms make up twenty-one percent of the Gospel accounts of Jesus' ministry." Mary Healy, *Healing: Bringing the Gift of God's Mercy to the World* (Huntington, IN: Our Sunday Visitor, 2015), 26.

10 See below for citations.

11 Pope Benedict XVI, *Jesus of Nazareth: From the Baptism in the Jordan to the Transfiguration* (New York: Doubleday, 2007), 47.

12 Mary Healy, *The Gospel of Mark*, Catholic Commentary on Sacred Scripture (Grand Rapids, MI: Baker Academic, 2008), 218. In fact, He seems to confirm the

title publicly by healing the blind man in fulfillment of messianic prophecy: "In that day . . ., out of their gloom and darkness the eyes of the blind shall see" (Isaiah 29:18; see also 35:5).

13   We also see the Cross connected profoundly to both.

14   That is, the throne of the cross.

15   See Isaiah 26:19; 29:18; 35:5-6; 42:18.

16   "If you diligently hearken to the voice of the Lord your God, and do that which is right in his eyes, and give heed to his commandments and keep all his statutes, I will put none of the diseases upon you which I put upon the Egyptians; for I am the Lord, your healer" (Exodus 15:26). "He lifts up the soul and gives light to the eyes; he grants healing, life, and blessing" (Sirach 34:17). "Behold, I will bring to [Jerusalem] health and healing, and I will heal them and reveal to them abundance of prosperity and security" (Jeremiah 33:6). "For you who fear my name the sun of righteousness shall rise, with healing in its wings" (Malachi 4:2).

17   In fact, in the Gospels, "to save" and "to raise up" have double meanings, referring both to physical healing and to complete salvation; see also James 5:14-15. See Congregation for the Doctrine of the Faith, *Instruction on Prayers for Healing*, September 14, 2000, 3; see also Healy, *Healing*, 119. Furthermore, both are connected to faith: faith saves and heals; it raises people up from the sick bed and raises people up to eternal life.

18   Pope Benedict XVI wrote, "Healings are essentially 'signs' that point to God himself and serve to set man in motion toward God. . . . For Jesus himself and for his followers, miracles of healing are thus a subordinate element within the overall range of his activity, which is concerned with something deeper, with nothing less than the 'Kingdom of God': his becoming Lord in us and in the world. . . . [We] must see [man] in his wholeness and must know that his ultimate healing can only be God's love." Pope Benedict XVI, *Jesus of Nazareth*, 176-177.

19   But sometimes, we see, when signs do not elicit faith they become occasions of God's judgment. In Matthew we read, "Woe to you, Chorazin! Woe to you Bethsaida! For if the mighty works done in you had been done in Tyre and Sidon, they would have repented long ago in sackcloth and ashes" (Matthew 11:20-21). In John, we read, "'If you are the Christ, tell us plainly.' Jesus answered them, 'I told you and you do not believe. The works that I do in my Father's name, they bear witness to me; but you do not believe, because you do not belong to my sheep'" (John 10:25).

20   See also appendix B, Frequently Asked Questions: *How do we know when to seek healing through prayer, and when to embrace or resign ourselves to redemptive suffering?*

21   Following the teaching of Christ, St. James explains how doubt hinders a person's ability to receive from the Lord: "Ask in faith, with no doubting, for he who doubts is like a wave of the sea that is driven and tossed by the wind. For that person must not suppose that a double-minded man, unstable in all his ways, will receive anything from the Lord" (James 1:6-7). Later, he explains how failure to pray, sin, and sinful passions, too, can hinder one's hopes/prayers: "You do not have, because you do not ask. You ask and do not receive, because you ask wrongly, to spend it

on your passions. Unfaithful creatures! Do you not know that friendship with the world is enmity with God? . . . Submit yourselves therefore to God. Resist the devil and he will flee from you. Draw near to God and he will draw near to you. Cleanse your hands, you sinners, and purify your hearts, you men of double mind" (James 4:2-4, 7-8). That sin hinders prayer is clear. But what about lack of faith? What is the actual connection between our faith and miracles? St. Thomas Aquinas answers: "The working of miracles is ascribed to faith . . . because it proceeds from God's omnipotence on which faith relies." *Summa Theologiae* II-II, Q. 178, Art. 1, ad. 5. In other words, God chooses to manifest his power especially to those who rely on it.

22 Jesus sent out not only the twelve apostles, the foundation stones of his kingdom, but also seventy-two disciples (Luke 10), bringing to mind the seventy-two elders who were given a share of the spirit to help Moses govern the people of Israel in the desert. At the end of this episode, Moses expresses his wish that all of the Lord's people would receive the Spirit of God (see Numbers 11:24-29). This eventuality is prophesied (Joel 2:28-29), and finally is fulfilled in the age of the Church, at Pentecost (Acts 2:1-13). Evidently, potentially any Christian can share in the gift of healing.

23 Among the commissions given by Jesus in Scripture, the "Great Commission" at the end of the Gospel of Matthew does not include explicit reference to healing and other miraculous signs; however, Jesus does have the apostles teach the people "to observe all that I have commanded you" (Matthew 28:20), which, from other teachings of his, we know includes performing signs and wonders through him.

24 Other than the evangelization of those who have never heard the gospel, Pope St. John Paul II identified two kinds of evangelization: the continuing evangelization of fervent Christians, and the re-evangelization of baptized persons who have fallen away from the practice of the faith (the "new evangelization"). John Paul II, *Redemptoris Missio* (On the Permanent Validity of the Church's Missionary Mandate), December 7, 1990, 33.

25 à Lapide, *The Holy Gospel According to Saint Mark*, The Great Commentary of Cornelius à Lapide (Fitzwilliam, NH: Loreto Publications, 2008), 110.

26 Irenaeus, *Against Heresies* 2.32.4, http://www.newadvent.org/fathers/0103232.htm.

27 Sulpitius Severus, *On the Life of St. Martin* 16, http://www.newadvent.org/fathers/3501.htm.

28 Healy, *Healing*, 55.

29 A close reading of Chrysostom leaves some doubt as to whether he, in fact, thought miracles had completely ceased, though it may seem at first glance that he did. John Chrysostom, *Homily 29 on First Corinthians*, 1, http://www.newadvent.org/fathers/220129.htm; John Chrysostom, Homily 8 on Colossians, http://www.newadvent.org/fathers/230308.htm. Augustine, in *De Vere Religione*, 25.47, written early on in his career, seems to say that miracles had completely ceased. However, in a much later work, he explains that this was not what he had meant: "When hands are laid on in Baptism people do not receive the Holy Spirit in such a way that they speak with the tongues of all the nations. Nor are the sick now healed by the shadow of Christ's preachers as they pass by. Clearly such things which happened then have later ceased. But I should not be understood to mean that

to-day no miracles are to be believed to happen in the name of Christ. For when I wrote that book I myself had just heard that a blind man in Milan had received his sight beside the bodies of the Milanese martyrs Protasius and Gervasius. And many others happen even in these times, so that it is impossible to know them all or to enumerate those we do know." *Retractions*, 1.13.7.

30 John Chrysostom, *Homily 36 on First Corinthians 7*, http://www.newadvent.org/fathers/220136.htm.

31 See McCready, W. D., *Signs of Sanctity: Miracles in the Thought of Gregory the Great* (Toronto: Pontifical Institute of Medieval Studies, 1989).

32 See Healy, *Healing*, 61-62.

33 See Augustine, *Concerning the City of God Against the Pagans*, trans. Henry Bettenson (New York: Penguin Books, 1984), 1043 (22.8).

34 *The Confessions of Saint Augustine*, trans. F. J. Sheed (New York: Sheed and Ward, 1943), 191 (9.4).

35 Augustine, *City of God*, 1039 (22.8).

36 John Hardon, "The Miracles of St. Francis Xavier," *American Ecclesiastical Review* 127 (October 1952): 248-263, http://www.therealpresence.org/archives/Miracles/Miracles_005.htm.

37 Pope Benedict XVI, *Jesus of Nazareth*, 47.

38 Congregation for the Doctrine of the Faith, *Ardens Felicitatis* (*Instruction on Prayers for Healing*), 13, 15, http://www.vatican.va/roman_curia/congregations/cfaith/documents/rc_con_cfaith_doc_20001123_istruzione_en.html.

39 "Part of the plan laid out in God's providence is that we should fight strenuously against all sickness and carefully seek the blessings of good health." Pope Paul VI, *Ordo Unctionis Infirmorum eorumque Pastoralis Curae, Editio Typica*, Rituale Romanum, 3 (Vatican Polyglot Press, 1972).

40 *Ardens Felicitatis*, 9.

41 Second Vatican Council, *Gaudium et Spes* (The Pastoral Constitution on the Church in the Modern World), December 7, 1965, 4.

42 Furthermore, we need to be careful when making comparisons of this kind. Most of us know very little about ages past, and even those who know much more will still find it difficult to enter into the minds of people of past centuries to get a more-or-less accurate sense of what it must have been like. We should not claim too much.

43 There were of course, many evils and disorders in medieval Christendom, as there are in every time and place. The point here is that today, society as a whole, in the Western world, has largely rejected God; and this can only lead to greater disorders.

44 Pope John Paul II, *Redemptoris Missio*, 3. The pope says this immediately after having mentioned the great decline in the Church, the increasing of "those who do not know Christ and do not belong to the Church."

45 *Redemptoris Missio*, 3.

46 Luckily for us; for that would be a difficult task.

47 Second Vatican Council, *Dei Verbum* (Dogmatic Constitution on Divine Revelation), November 18, 1965, 2.

48 There have been churchmen, even saints and Fathers of the Church, who appeared to hold an opinion resembling or approaching the "cessationist" one. In the first chapter, on healing in Scripture and the early Church, we saw that St. John Chrysostom was among them.

49 First Vatican Council, *Dei Filius* (Dogmatic Constitution on the Catholic Faith), April 24, 1870, 3. See also Pius XII: "Members gifted with miraculous powers will never be lacking in the Church." *Mystici Corporis Christi* (Encyclical on the Mystical Body of Christ), June 29, 1943, 17.

50 See appendix B, Frequently Asked Questions: *Can't only holy people, like the saints, heal?*

51 Second Vatican Council, *Lumen Gentium* (Dogmatic Constitution on the Church), November 21, 1964, 40.

52 Second Vatican Council, *Apostolicam Actuositatem* (Decree on the Apostolate of the Laity), November 18, 1965, 2.

53 Charismatic gifts exist alongside hierarchical gifts. Both are given to the Church for the common good: "The Church, which the Spirit guides in way of all truth and which He unified in communion and in works of ministry, He both equips and directs with hierarchical and charismatic gifts and adorns with His fruits." *Lumen Gentium*, 4. Charismatic and hierarchical gifts are "co-essential" to the Church. See Congregation for the Doctrine of the Faith, *Iuvenescit Ecclesia* (Letter to the Bishops of the Catholic Church Regarding the Relationship Between Hierarchical and Charismatic Gifts in the Life and the Mission of the Church), May 15, 2016, 10.

54 *Apostolicam Actuositatem*, 3.

55 *Lumen Gentium*, 12. The *Catechism of the Catholic Church* teaches the same: "Grace is first and foremost the gift of the Spirit who justifies and sanctifies us. But grace also includes the gifts that the Spirit grants us to associate us with his work, to enable us to collaborate in the salvation of others and in the growth of the body of Christ, the Church. There are sacramental graces, gifts proper to the different sacraments. There are furthermore special graces, also called charisms after the Greek term used by St. Paul and meaning 'favor,' 'gratu¬itous gift,' 'benefit.' Whatever their character—sometimes it is extraordinary, such as the gift of miracles or of tongues—charisms are oriented toward sanctifying grace and are intended for the common good of the Church. They are at the service of char¬ity which builds up the Church" (2003).

56 Congregation for the Doctrine of the Faith, *Instruction on Prayers for Healing*, September 14, 2000, 5.

57 John Paul II, *Message to the participants of the World Congress of Ecclesial Movements promoted by the Pontifical Council for the Laity*, May 27, 1998, 5.

58 John Paul II, *Speech to Ecclesial Movements and New Communities*, May 10, 1998, 5.

59 *Iuvenescit Ecclesia*, 9.

60 *Lumen Gentium*, 12 (Abbot translation). Because of other, incomplete English translations, which fail to include the word, "rashly," some incorrectly believe that the Vatican II document *Lumen Gentium* forbids praying for extraordinary charisms like healing. However the official Latin text of the document includes the word, "temere," which is translated "rashly."

61 See also appendix B, Frequently Asked Questions: *What does it mean to "rashly" seek extraordinary gifts of the Holy Spirit?*

62 The complete quote, Flannery translation: "Extraordinary gifts are not to be sought after [rashly], nor are the fruits of apostolic labor to be presumptuously expected from their use; but judgment as to their genuinity and proper use belongs to those who are appointed leaders in the Church, to whose special competence it belongs, not indeed to extinguish the Spirit, but to test all things and hold fast to that which is good." *Lumen Gentium*, 12.

63 We will refer to this episode again in chapter 4, "Praying for the Gifts."

64 *Instruction on Prayers for Healing*, 1.

65 Augustine, *Sermon 38.2*, as quoted in Mary Healy, *Healing*, 63.

66 To apply to simple emotional conditions such as anger, anxiety, and depression, see appendix A, Extra Topics.

67 See, for example, Mary Healy, "A Model for Healing Prayer," in *Healing*.

68 Sometimes Christ himself did this. See Mark 9:21, 10:51.

69 See appendix C, Praying for Specific Conditions.

70 See appendix A, Extra Topics, for more. Many require deeper emotional and spiritual healing than is usually possible in the context of public evangelization, and/or require more qualified help. It is important to recognize when you are out of your depth.

71 See appendix B, Frequently Asked Questions: *Are laypeople allowed to lay hands on others? Do we always need to lay hands on people? What about laying hands on sensitive areas?*

72 See appendix B, Extra Topics: *Forgiveness and Repentance.*

73 "Orans," which means "praying" in Latin, is also an ancient Christian prayer posture used by the faithful in private prayer, by priests at Mass, and is often seen in icons of the Blessed Virgin Mary and other saints, in which the elbows are held close to the sides of the body with the hands outstretched sideways, palms up.

74 See appendix B, Frequently Asked Questions: *Do we always need to lay hands on people? What about laying hands on sensitive areas?*

75 They may also experience a change in the location, type, or severity of the pain. See appendix B, Frequently Asked Questions: What if the pain moves or increases during healing prayer?

76 They may even receive a healing earlier, while you call upon the Holy Spirit.

77   See *The Catholic Encyclopedia*, s.v. "Adjuration," http://www.newadvent.org/cathen/01142c.htm; ST II-II, Q.90.

78   See appendix B, Frequently Asked Questions: *Adjuration: Is it ok to command the body? To command demons?*

79   See appendix B, Frequently Asked Questions: *What is a "spirit of affliction?"*

80   Evil spirits can at times be a cause behind certain ailments, so that when they are driven out, the ailment goes with them. "In the name of Jesus, I command any spirit of affliction to leave now. I command any spirit of pain to leave now, in the name of Jesus." This is more likely to be the case when an illness seems connected to emotional wounds or sins that have not been repented of. See appendix B, Frequently Asked Questions: *What is a "spirit of affliction?"* See also appendix A, Extra Topics: *Deliverance Prayer.*

81   "It is quite common for those who devoutly cling to God to work miracles in both of these ways … either through their prayers or by their own power, as circumstances may dictate." Gregory the Great, *Dialogues 2.30, in "Life and Miracles of St. Benedict (Book Two of the Dialogues),"* trans. Odo J. Zimmermann and Benedict R. Avery (Collegeville, MN: The Liturgical Press, 1984), 61.

82   Conditions which are readily able to be tested for improvements include any condition where pain or discomfort is involved, such as injuries resulting in back pain, joint pain, or neck pain, but also other conditions with pain or discomfort, like pneumonia or cancer. It also includes conditions involving joint stiffness, the inability to move in certain ways, and the hindrance of other bodily organs like in blindness, deafness, or the inability to smell, and conditions visible to the eye, like warts, boils, tumors, and rashes.

83   See appendix A, Extra Topics.

84   See appendix B, Frequently Asked Questions: *What if the illness or injury comes back?*

85   *Catechism of the Catholic Church*, 1266, 1268, 1270, 1302–1303, 1305.

86   *Catechism*, 1128.

87   Especially *Summa Theologiae* III, Q. 66-69, 71. See also Ralph Martin, "The Post-Christendom Sacramental Crisis: The Wisdom of Thomas Aquinas," Nova et Vetera 11, no. 1 (2013): 65-70, https://www.renewalministries.net/files/freeliterature/novaetvetera11_1martin_(2).pdf.

88   Tertullian, *On Baptism* 20, http://www.newadvent.org/fathers/0321.htm.

89   Hilary of Poitiers, *Tract on the Psalms* 64.15, quoted in Kilian McDonnell and George T. Montague, *Christian Initiation and Baptism in the Holy Spirit: Evidence from the First Eight Centuries*, 2nd ed. (Collegeville, MN: Liturgical Press, 1994), 184, 186.

90   See *Catechism* teaching on the charisms, esp. paragraphs 798–801, and 2003–2004. See also paragraphs 1506–1509 for teaching on the charism of healing.

91   See Cornelius à Lapide, Saint Paul's First and Second Epistles to the Corinthians, The Great Commentary of Cornelius à Lapide (Fitzwilliam, NH: Loreto Publications, 2016), 324; see also 299. In St. Thomas Aquinas's commentary on 1

Corinthians 14:1, he says simply that we should love the charisms and be zealous for them: "And this is what he says: earnestly desire the spiritual gifts. As if to say: Although charity is greater than all gifts, nevertheless the others are not to be despised. But earnestly desire, i.e., fervently love the spiritual gifts of the Holy Spirit. . . . [Again] he says: especially that you may prophecy. As if to say: Among spiritual gifts be more zealous for the gift of prophecy." Thomas Aquinas, *St. Thomas Aquinas: Commentary on the First Epistle to the Corinthians* (Kindle Locations 3469–3471, 3480–3481), Kindle Edition. However, it is hard to imagine how St. Thomas (let alone St. Paul) could say that one is to "fervently love" and be zealous for a gift if he thought that it shouldn't ever be prayed for.

92 See appendix B, Frequently Asked Questions: *Isn't it true that we're not supposed to seek out extraordinary gifts?*

93 Second Vatican Council, *Lumen Gentium* [Dogmatic Constitution on the Church], November 21, 1964, sec. 12. Abbot Translation. See appendix B, Frequently Asked Questions: *What does it mean to "rashly" seek extraordinary gifts of the Holy Spirit?*

94 See John 20:21-22; Acts 8:14-19, 19:6; 1 Timothy 4:14; 2 Timothy 1:6; Numbers 11:16-18; Deuteronomy 34:9. The impartation of gifts through the sacraments is mostly the domain of the clergy, and they confer spiritual gifts in an official and uniquely efficacious manner as ordained ministers. Bishops and priests serve in the person of Christ the head of the Church, and in the name of the whole Church. See *Catechism*, 875–876, 1548–1553.

95 As seen in the examples we provide, the reception of gifts in a non-sacramental context for the building up of the Church, occurs through both clergy and laity. When done so by laity, it must be done in cooperation and communion with the clergy. See *Catechism*, 910, 913, 951.

96 Mary Kathleen Glavich, *Therese of Lisieux: The Way of Love* (Boston: Pauline Books and Media, 2003), 77.

97 Bert Ghezzi, *Mystics and Miracles: True Stories of Lives Touched by God* (Chicago: Loyola Press, 2002), 173.

98 Don't mistake "losing heart" for God telling you to stop praying!

99 John of the Cross, *The Collected Works of St. John of the Cross*, Revised Edition, trans. Kieran Kavanaugh and Otilio Rodriguez (Washington, D.C.: Institute of Carmelite Studies), 324-325; see 324-328.

100 Ibid., 325.

101 Ibid., 324.

102 Paul VI, *Evangelii Nuntiandi* (Apostolic Exhortation on Evangelization in the Modern World), December 8, 1975, 75.

103 John Paul II, *Veritatis Splendor* (Encyclical Regarding Certain Fundamental Questions of the Church's Moral Teaching), August 6, 1993, 108.

104 Here is one example of a daily offering prayer: "Eternal Father, I offer You everything I do this day: my work, my prayers, my apostolic efforts; my time with family and friends; my hours of relaxation; my difficulties, problems, distress, which

I shall try to bear with patience. Join these, my gifts, to the unique offering which Jesus Christ, Your Son, renews today in the Eucharist. Grant, I pray, that, vivified by the Holy Spirit and united to the Sacred Heart of Jesus and the Immaculate Heart of Mary, my life this day may be of service to you and your children and help consecrate the world to you. Amen." See The Apostleship of Prayer for more information and examples: http://www.popesprayerusa.net/daily-offering-prayers/.

105 "God our Father, I believe that out of your infinite love you have created me. In a thousand ways I have rejected your love. I repent of each and every one of my sins. Please forgive me. Thank you for sending your Son to die for me, to save me from eternal death. I choose this day to renew my covenant with you and to place Jesus at the center of my heart. I surrender to him as Lord over my whole life. I ask you now to flood my soul with the gift of the Holy Spirit, so that my life may be transformed. Give me the grace and courage to live as a disciple in your Church for the rest of my days. Amen." Holy cards can be purchased in bulk at our online store, http://streetevangelization.com/spse-store/product/holy-cards-consecration-to-the-sacred-heart/.

106 See John Paul II, *Novo Millennio Ineunte* (Apostolic Letter at the Close of the Great Jubilee of the Year 2000), January 6, 2001, sec. 16–17.

107 True, the Lord can use a non-rational beast as an instrument for his purposes, but the difference is whether we are to do the work of the Father more like a hammer in his hand or like a free and obedient daughter or son.

108 This is the path to holiness. For a great resource on the doctrine of the saints concerning the path to holiness, see Ralph Martin, *The Fulfillment of All Desire: A Guidebook for the Journey to God Based on the Wisdom of the Saints* (Steubenville, OH: Emmaus Road, 2006).

109 It is what the apostles preached: "What we preach is not ourselves, but Jesus Christ as Lord" (2 Corinthians 4:5).

110 *IChThYS: Iesous Christos Theou Yios Soter.*

111 If we were to answer new questions raised by all these things, and again, and so on, we would move on eventually to the whole of Christian doctrine; for the doctrines of the faith are all profoundly interconnected.

112 Paul VI, *Evangelii Nuntiandi*, 10.

113 Paul VI, *Evangelii Nuntiandi*, 27–28.

114 The great usefulness of personal testimony is connected to this truth. Your personal testimony explains how Jesus has been savior to you, in the concrete conditions of your life, through the truths of the Christian life. This can give hope to those who hear that Jesus can be savior to them, too.

115 Appealing to their implicit knowledge of God through their worship of "an unknown god," St. Paul focuses on preaching about the identity of the one true God, and then moves on to speak of the judgment, Jesus Christ, the need for repentance, and the confirmation of this message by the resurrection.

116 Here, St. Paul spends his time arguing from the Old Testament Scriptures that the Messiah was to suffer, and that Jesus is the Messiah. It is obvious and presumed that the Messiah is Savior.

117 Preaching the kingdom, which was the salvation they hoped for; and telling parables about the kingdom that related to their experience.

118 Using the symbolism of the water she was seeking, he appeals to her inner thirst for eternal life, and brings to light her insatiable search for love in a string of sinful relationships, and to the need to worship God rightly. He presents himself as Savior; that is, the One who can quench her thirst, and bring her truth and eternal life.

119 The Old Testament, too, for that matter.

120 There is a reason that immediately after giving the apostles the commission to preach the gospel and baptize, Jesus commissions them also to teach life in him: "Go therefore and make disciples of all nations . . . teaching them to observe all that I have commanded you" (Matthew 28:19-20).

121 Augustine, *Confessions*, trans. Henry Chadwick (New York: Oxford University Press, 1998), 3 (1.1).

122 Yet this will is mysterious. The same God who desires all to be saved also "has mercy upon whomever he wills, and . . . hardens the heart of whomever he wills" (Romans 9:18). When he hardens the hearts of some, we can have hope that in the long run, his designs on their lives will lead to salvation, for "where sin increased, grace abounded all the more" (Romans 5:20), and "They have now been disobedient in order that by the mercy shown to you they also may receive mercy. For God has consigned all men to disobedience, that he may have mercy upon all" (Romans 11:30-32). When evangelization efforts fail, we "shake the dust off of our feet" but rely on prayer and sacrifice because no person is without hope until after their last breath (See Matthew 20:1-16).

123 We can see this from Acts alone. Peter referred to God's judgment in his kerygmatic preaching in Acts 2:20; 3:23; and 10:42. Paul in Acts 13:40-41; and 17:30-31. The specific doctrine of hell appears in Jesus' teaching in the Gospels, as well as in James 3:6, and 2 Peter 2:4. In addition, Paul refers to the judgment many times in his letters.

124 See *Catechism*, 1453; Robert I. Bradley, and Eugene Kevane, trans., *The Roman Catechism*: Translated and Annotated in Accord with Vatican II and Post-Conciliar Documents and the New Code of Canon Law (Boston, MA: St. Paul Editions, 1985), 258–259; and ST II-II Q.19, for a more complete treatment. St. Thomas calls this fear of punishment "servile fear," even when it loses its servile character in those who have been regenerated by sanctifying grace. The term, therefore, may be confusing, and since it has bad connotations for most people, it should not normally be used.

125 Attributed to St. Francis de Sales. See http://www.catholicworldreport.com/2017/11/18/we-must-fear-god-from-love-not-love-god-from-fear/.

126 The belief that all or nearly all will be saved, simply as a matter of course.

127 For a worthwhile book on these and closely related topics, see Ralph Martin, *Will Many Be Saved?: What Vatican II Actually Teaches and Its Implications for the New Evangelization* (Grand Rapids, MI: Eerdmans, 2012).

128 A work which he is already carrying out independently of our efforts.

129 Catherine of Siena, *Dialogue* IV, 138, in *Catechism*, 313.

130 Thereby committing "blasphemy against the Holy Spirit." See *Catechism*, 1864.

131 This does not mean, however, that you will not reason or use arguments. Obviously, from his letters it is clear that St. Paul himself did. But you ought not to use reason in a way that relies on it in preference to the grace of God. Your reason must be at the service of grace, and grace will conquer all worldly prudence and philosophy (See 2 Corinthians 10:1-6).

132 "Evangelization loses much of its force and effectiveness if it does not take into consideration the actual people to whom it is addressed . . . but on the other hand, evangelization risks losing its power and disappearing altogether if one empties or adulterates its content." Paul VI, *Evangelii Nuntiandi*, 63.

133 Paul VI, *Evangelii Nuntiandi*, 22.

134 It should go without saying that in all of this, avoid "speaking down" to them or treating them as ignorant.

135 Sometimes Mass may not be the best shallow entry point for a non-Catholic. If the person is not a Catholic, and you do think that the beauty of the Mass might help them along, give them instruction on what to expect at Mass, and how they should conduct themselves.

136 See ST II-II, Q. 30, Art. 4.

137 ST II-II, Q. 30, Art. 1. This translation of the text comes from Alfred J. Freddoso, *New English Translation of St. Thomas Aquinas's Summa Theologiae*, https://www3.nd.edu/~afreddos/summa-translation/Part%202-2/st2-2-ques30.pdf.

138 "The sum total of the Christian religion consists in mercy, as regards external works." ST II-II, Q. 30, Art. 4, ad. 2.

139 Our online store is a great source for affordable medals and holy cards in bulk. Go to http://streetevangelization.com/spse-store/.

140 *Catechism*, 905.

141 *Catechism*, 1816.

142 We told this story in more detail at the beginning of the second chapter.

143 See appendix A, Extra Topics: *The Charism of Prophecy*.

144 This is a more-detailed account of a story also told in the recent Urban Ministries Productions Documentary "Fearless." https://www.fearlessdocumentary.net/.

145 Basil the Great, On the Holy Spirit 26.61, http://www.newadvent.org/fathers/3203.htm.

146 Sec. 30, http://www.newadvent.org/fathers/01282.htm

147 When Jesus commissioned his twelve apostles and seventy (or seventy-two) disciples to preach the gospel and heal, he also commissioned them to drive away demons (See Luke 9:1-2, 10:17-20). The apostles, of course, are succeeded by the order of bishops. The seventy (or seventy-two) disciples are traditionally understood to be succeeded by the order of priests. Cornelius à Lapide, The Holy Gospel According to Saint Luke, The Great Commentary of Cornelius à Lapide (Fitzwilliam, NH: Loreto Publications, 2008), 431.

148 Thus, St. Paul makes truth, righteousness, the gospel, faith, salvation, and the Word of God the armor we must wear in the battle against the evil one and his minions: "We are not contending against flesh and blood, but . . . against the spiritual hosts of wickedness. . . . Therefore take the whole armor of God, that you may be able to withstand in the evil day, and having done all, to stand. Stand therefore, having girded your loins with truth, and having put on the breastplate of righteousness, and having shod your feet with the equipment of the gospel of peace; above all taking the shield of faith, with which you can quench all the flaming darts of the evil one. And take the helmet of salvation, and the sword of the Spirit, which is the word of God. Pray at all times in the Spirit, with all prayer and supplication. To that end keep alert with all perseverance, making supplication for all the saints" (Ephesians 6:12-18).

149 For a collection of prayers for deliverance, see *Prayers Against the Powers of Darkness* (USCCB, 2017), which is the official English translation of appendix B of the ritual book used by exorcists in the modern exorcism rite; also Fr. Chad Ripperger's *Deliverance Prayers: For Use by the Laity* (CreateSpace, 2016).

150 See Ripperger, *Deliverance Prayers*, 8.

151 Under no circumstances should a layperson ask any questions of a demon or speak to it directly in any way except to adjure it to leave. They should refer serious cases to a priest. See appendix B, Frequently Asked Questions: *Adjuration: Is it ok to command the body? And to command demons?*

152 Origen, *Contra Celsus*, 8.27. http://www.newadvent.org/fathers/04168.htm.

153 The First Part of the Second Part, Question 111.

154 The Second Part of the Second Part, Questions 171 through 178.

155 ST I-II, Q. 111, Art. 4. Charisms are given "that a man may help another to be led to God." ST I-II Q. 111, Art. 1.

156 ST II-II, pr. Q. 171. There, in the treatise on gratuitous graces, the knowledge classification of the charisms includes faith, wisdom, knowledge, discernment of spirits, interpretation of tongues (mentioned in a reply to an objection), and prophecy; the action (operation) classification includes miraculous deeds and healing; and the speech classification includes tongues, the word of knowledge, and the word of wisdom. In the treatise on grace, on the other hand, the class of knowledge includes faith, wisdom, discernment of spirits, knowledge, and prophecy; the class of action (operation) includes miraculous deeds, healing, prophecy, and discernment of spirits; and the class of speech includes tongues and interpretation of tongues. Whatever St. Thomas's reasons for classifying them in different ways, it seems that the difference reflects the richness and interconnectedness of the gifts.

157 This refers not to the knowledge of "general and obscure infused contemplation" which is part of growth in virtues, the seven-fold gifts of the Holy Spirit, and sanctifying grace, but "different modes of particular and distinct supernatural knowledge," according to a distinction made by St. John of the Cross. Reginald Garrigou-Lagrange, *The Three Ages of the Interior Life: Prelude of Eternal Life* (Rockford, IL: Tan Books and Publishers, 1989), 2:578.

158 ST II-II, Q. 171, Art. 1. In line with this broad vision of the prophecy, St. Thomas argues that Moses was the greatest of the prophets because he possessed the enlightenment of knowledge and confirming miracles to very excellent degrees. ST II-II, Q. 174, Art. 4; see Deuteronomy 34:10-12.

159 In the more narrow sense of prophesying the future by declaring what is sure to come to pass, or some word from the Lord giving hope, encouragement, or warning. (In a sense these also concern the future, in that they concern what may come to pass.)

160 There are other elements of St. Thomas' accounts of the charisms, besides those that we have outlined, that lead us to see all-the-more that they are interconnected, ordered to the same goal, and united under the heading of "prophecy": between his treatises on grace and on gratuitous graces, St. Thomas classifies the gifts according to the three-fold schema in a couple different ways, and seems to interpret individual gifts them in various or multi-faceted ways.

161 Depending on how you define the various charisms listed in 1 Corinthians 12:8-11, Patrick's "promptings," "senses," and imaginative images could be characterized specifically as words of wisdom and knowledge, or as prophecy, or even in one case as discernment of spirits, in that he was given to manifest a secret of Willie's heart. A recent, helpful resource for understanding one perspective on the meaning of the different charisms is Randy Clark and Mary Healy, The Spiritual Gifts Handbook: Using Your Gifts to Build the Kingdom (Bloomington, MN: Chosen Books, 2018).

162 Second Vatican Council, Dei Verbum (Dogmatic Constitution on Divine Revelation), November 18, 1965, 2.

163 "Christ is the first and chief teacher of spiritual doctrine and faith. . . . Hence it is clear that all the gratuitous graces were most excellently in Christ." ST III, Q. 7, Art. 7.

164 Catechism, 436.

165 All the faithful of whatever rank share in the prophetic office of Christ, together with the priestly and royal offices. Catechism, 871–873. The laity's prophetic role commits them to evangelization. Catechism, 904–907.

166 It seems significant that the most miraculous figures of the Old Testament are Moses and Elijah, for they are the two great representatives of "the Law and the Prophets" fulfilled by Christ, appearing with Him on the mountain of the transfiguration.

167 Apostolic Constitutions, 8.1. http://www.newadvent.org/fathers/07158.htm.

168 See Summa Theologiae II-II, Q. 178, art. 2.

169 John of the Cross, The Collected Works of St. John of the Cross, Revised Edition, trans. Kieran Kavanaugh and Otilio Rodriguez (Washington, DC: Institute of Carmelite Studies), 213.

170 Though we may receive them, we must not let ourselves make too much of them or trust them, or be attached to them; instead, we should simply reveal them to our spiritual directors, and accept whatever good spirit of devotion they may have brought us, "putting into practice . . . whatever is for the service of God," and then move on. John of the Cross, The Collected Works, 209.

171 "There is no reason to delay in giving signs for the discernment of good visions from bad ones. . . . My sole intention here is to instruct the intellect about them so that it may not be hindered and impeded from union with divine wisdom by the good ones, nor deceived by the false ones." John of the Cross, *The Collected Works*, 201.

172 John of the Cross, *The Collected Works*, 238.

173 See John of the Cross, *The Collected Works*, 324-328.

174 John of the Cross, *The Collected Works*, 324.

175 John of the Cross, *The Collected Works*, 294.

176 St. Thomas Aquinas expresses this well in his commentary on St. Paul: "Then when he says, But earnestly, he rectifies their affection for the above spiritual gifts, saying: Since there are many gifts of the Holy Spirit, earnestly desire the higher gifts, namely, have a stronger desire for the better graces; for example, prophecy than the gift of tongues, as will be said below (13:1); 'Test everything; hold fast what is good' (1 Th 5:21). And in order that their affections may not come to rest in the above-mentioned gifts, he adds: I will show you a still more excellent way, namely, the way of charity, by which one goes to God in a more direct way: 'I will run in the way of thy commandments' (Ps 119:32); 'This is the way, walk in it' (Is 30:21)." Thomas Aquinas, *St. Thomas Aquinas: Commentary On the First Epistle to the Corinthians* (Kindle Locations 3147–3152), Kindle Edition.

177 For an example, see à Lapide, *Epistles to Corinthians*, 299, 324. Also, Tertullian wrote, "Therefore, blessed ones, whom the grace of God awaits, when you ascend from that most sacred font of your new birth, and spread your hands for the first time in the house of your mother, together with your brethren, ask from the Father, ask from the Lord, that His own specialties of grace and distributions of gifts may be supplied you. Ask, says He, and you shall receive." *On Baptism* 20, http://www.newadvent.org/fathers/0321.htm.

178 Second Vatican Council, *Lumen Gentium* (Dogmatic Constitution on the Church), November 21, 1964, 12.

179 Other spirits may produce other kinds of effects in a person: a "spirit of divination" (Acts 16:16), a "lying spirit" (1 Kings 22:20-22), etc.

180 See Thomas Aquinas, *Summa Theologiae* II-II, q.90, art. 1-3, http://www.newadvent.org/summa/3090.htm.

181 Authorized priests engage in limited conversation with demons in the official rite of exorcism, but laity are not permitted to do so. See Congregation for the Doctrine of the Faith, *Letter to Ordinaries regarding norms on Exorcism*, http://www.vatican.va/roman_curia/congregations/cfaith/documents/rc_con_cfaith_doc_19850924_exorcism_en.html.

182 *The Catholic Encyclopedia*, s.v. "aduration," http://www.newadvent.org/cathen/01142c.htm.

183 Gabriele Amorth, *An Exorcist: More Stories* (San Francisco: Ignatius Press, 2002), 91-92.

184 Congregation for the Doctrine of the Faith, *Instruction on Prayers for Healing*, September 14, 2000, 1.

185 "Suppose I fall sick of a malignant fever. In this event, I see that it is God's good pleasure that I should be quite indifferent as to whether I am ill or well; but the known will of God is that I should call in a doctor and apply all the remedies possible (I do not say the very best remedies, but the common and ordinary ones). God has shown this to us by giving healing power to remedies; Holy Scripture in various places teaches us to do so; and the Church commands it." Francis de Sales, *The Art of Loving God: Simple Virtues for the Christian Life* (Manchester, NH: Sophia Institute Press, 1998), 16.

186 Augustine, *Letter* 130, VI, 13.

187 Basil the Great, *On the Holy Spirit* 26.61, http://www.newadvent.org/fathers/3203.htm.

188 Hilary of Poitiers, *Tract on the Psalms* 64.15, quoted in Kilian McDonnell and George T. Montague, *Christian Initiation and Baptism in the Holy Spirit: Evidence from the First Eight Centuries*, 2nd ed. (Collegeville, MN: Liturgical Press, 1994), 184, 186.

189 John Paul II, *Pastores Dabo Vobis* (On the Formation of Priests in the Circumstances of the Present Day), 31.

190 ST II-II, Q. 178, Art. 2.

191 See appendix A, Extra Topics: *Emotional and Spiritual Healing*; Deliverance Prayer.